The Secret War in the Sudan: 1955–1972

EDGAR O'BALLANCE

ARCHON BOOKS
Hamden, Connecticut

First published in 1977
by Faber and Faber Limited
3 Queen Square London WC1N 3AU
and in the United States of America as an
Archon Book, an imprint of The Shoe String Press, Inc.
Hamden, Connecticut 06514
All rights reserved

Library of Congress Cataloging in Publication Data

O'Ballance, Edgar.
 The secret war in the Sudan, 1955–1972.

 Includes bibliographical references and index.
 1. Sudan—History—1956–   I. Title.
DT108.7.022 1977   962.4′05   77–1732
ISBN 0–208–01692–9

Printed in Great Britain

The Secret War in the Sudan: 1955–1972

by the same author

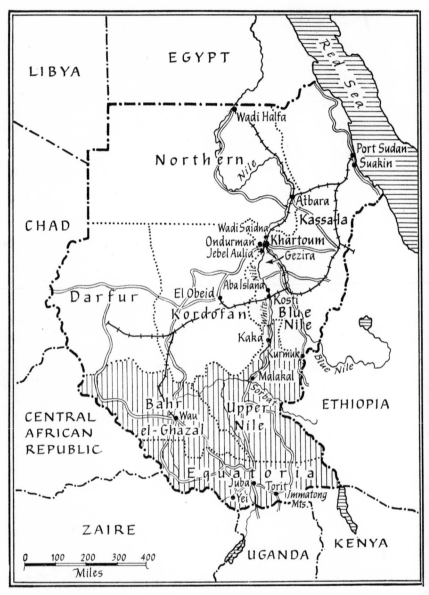

General map of the Sudan, showing the adjacent countries

Contents

Contents

Acknowledgements

The information contained in this book has been obtained from my own interviewing, research, correspondence with various personalities, and my travels in the Sudan and elsewhere, but I should like to record that I have read with profit and pleasure the following works, and I would like to make my grateful acknowledgements to the authors, compilers or editors:

Albino, Oliver: *The Sudan: A Southern Viewpoint*, Oxford University Press (1970)

Baker, Anne: *Morning Star*, William Kimber (1972)

Beshire, Mohammed Omer: *The Southern Sudan: Background to Conflict*, Hurst, London (1968)

Eprile, Cecil: *War & Peace in the Sudan: 1955–1972*, David & Charles (1974)

——: *Sudan: the Long War*, Conflict Study: March 1972, Institute for the Study of Conflict

Furst, Ruth: *The Barrel of a Gun*, Allen Lane, Penguin Press (1971)

Henderson, K. D. D.: *The Sudan Republic*, Ernest Benn (1965)

Holt, P. M.: *A Modern History of the Sudan*, Weidenfeld & Nicolson (1961)

Kinross, Lord: *Portrait of Egypt*, Andre Deutsch (1966)

MacMichael, Sir Harold: *The Sudan*, Ernest Benn (1954)

Mahgoub, Mohammed Ahmed: *Democracy on Trial*, Andre Deutsch (1974)

Martin, David: *General Amin*, Faber & Faber (1974)

Moorehead, Alan: *The Blue Nile*, Hamish Hamilton (1962)

——: *The White Nile*, Hamish Hamilton (1962)

Morrison, Godfrey: *The Southern Sudan and Eritrea*, Minority Rights Group pamphlet (1974)

Acknowledgements

Uduhu, Joseph, and William Deng: *Problem of the Southern Sudan*, O.U.P. (1963)

Wai, Dunstan M (Edited by): *The Southern Sudan: The Problem of National Integration*, Frank Cass, London (1973)

Waterfield, Gordon: *Egypt*, Thames & Hudson (1967)

Yangu, Alexis Mbali: *The Nile Turns Red*, Pageant, New York (1966)

Grass Curtain: Edited by Mading de Garang: various issues

Basic Facts about the Southern Provinces of the Sudan: Government Information pamphlet: Khartoum (1964)

The US Army Area Handbook of the Republic of the Sudan: Department of the Army (August 1960)

Sudan Notes and Records (40 volumes): courtesy of the Khartoum Library

Abbreviations

ANAF	Anya-Nya Armed Forces
ALF	Azania Liberation Front
LFA	Land Freedom Army
NUP	National Unionist Party
OAU	Organization of African Unity
SACDNU	Sudan African Closed Districts National Union
SALF	Sudan African Liberation Front
SANU	Sudan African National Union
SSLM	South Sudan Liberation Movement
SSU	Sudan Socialist Union
UN	United Nations

Preface

Conducted on the now familiar revolutionary guerilla warfare pattern, and lasting from 1955 until 1972, the struggle in the southern Sudan was a 'secret war', news of which was deliberately suppressed by successive Sudanese governments which did not want the world to know about their southern problem. Governments of adjacent countries tried to ignore it too, and neither the UN nor the OAU were the least bit interested in the plight of the black southerners, of whom it is estimated that about half a million perished by the bullet, spear, land mine, famine or disease. The south was surrounded and smothered by a 'grass curtain' of silence, and it was only in the latter years of the war that this curtain was penetrated and some news trickled out.

This was the first time in modern history that black Africans had stood up and fought an Arab power. The northern part of the Sudan firmly considered itself to be Arab, although purists may hold divergent views on this. The southerners, mainly animist Negroes, wanted to be free from the harsh, unsympathetic rule of the Muslim northerners, but they eventually had to settle for less and accept a form of local autonomy.

It was a cruel war in which the civilian population suffered considerably from both armies, as villages were razed to the ground, over a million people were forced to flee from their homes, no prisoners were taken, and latterly Government aircraft dropped bombs on and fired rockets and machine guns at villages and camps. The two opposing armies, that of the north and that of the 'mutineers' and 'outlaws' (which came to be known as the Anya-Nya, meaning 'snake poison' in the local dialects), seemed to vie with each other in their ruthless measures against the population.

In an area of some 250,000 square miles of forest, swamp and scrub, with scanty communications, the Anya-Nya came to dominate the countryside, while the Government security forces, using aircraft and modern weapons, tried to hold on to the population centres and to keep the roads open. In other words, it was the classic guerilla impasse. There were no large battles, as the Anya-Nya were too elusive, but spasmodic flurries of ambushes, small actions and mine-laying.

The north had many drawbacks. It had a comparatively small army, for the size of the country and population, of never more than 40,000 men, of whom up to two-thirds were employed in the south. Considering that the usually accepted ratio of conventional troops required to defeat guerilla forces is in the order of 10:1, and that the north, especially at first, had few aircraft and vehicles, its forces were certainly not adequate to patrol and pacify such a huge expanse of terrain. The southerners had even more disadvantages, not the least being their mediocre and quarrelling leadership which held differing views on the aims to be achieved and the methods used. At one stage there were three southern 'governments' in the south and one in exile, together with three southern political parties in the north and one in exile, the majority claiming to speak solely for the whole of the south. Other disadvantages were lack of money, weapons, external support, and the traditional psychological feeling of inferiority when facing the Arabs, who for centuries had contemptuously regarded them as *abeed*, or slaves. But the vital disadvantage was the lack of a southern voice to penetrate the 'grass curtain' to tell the world of their plight and needs, and to enlist sympathy, encouragement and help. It was only in the final two years of the war, when the 'grass curtain' was pierced, that an indifferent world became uneasily aware of what was happening in southern Sudan.

In both camps since the cease fire there has been an atmosphere of reconciliation, of forgiving and forgetting. Both are reluctant to talk of the past and wish only to speak of the future. This attitude has made it difficult for me at times to obtain accurate details of various aspects and actions of the war, or to check certain reports or allegations. In many of the interviews I had with leading personalities, and others of lesser importance, answers tended to become vague and evasive when I tried to delve deeply into what had previously happened. General Lagu, usually a cheerful, frank and open personality, also has limits in this respect because of his concern for the implementation of the agreement and of common unity. And in one of his letters to me he wrote: 'It is best to forward such questions to me through the Government to avoid sensitivity.' This sums up the present climate, which is good for the future but bad for the probing historian.

The main lesson emerging from the grass curtain war—one which governments are slow to accept but which many revolutionary movements have long mastered—is that an efficient propaganda machine should have greater priority than guns, money or any other single factor.

The spelling of personal names, especially of southerners, has provided a minor problem. Mostly they have several, that include their tribal names, adopted names and those acquired at mission schools, not all of which they use at the same time or habitually. Izbone Mendiri Gwonzo, for example, is usually known as Izbone Mendiri, and Abel Alier Wal Kuai as simply Abel Alier. I have used the simpler and more popular form throughout.

EDGAR O'BALLANCE

1 *The Sudan: 1821–1936*

'Allah laughed when he created the Sudan.'

Arab proverb

Remote, unknown, a perpetual ancient wonder of the world as the source of the River Nile, land-locked, forest-locked and desert-locked, the three southern Sudanese provinces of present-day[1] Bahr el-Ghazal, Upper Nile and Equatoria for milleniums had little contact with the outside world, and their inhabitants remained in a primitive state. The medieval Arab name for the belt of territory that spread across Africa just south of the Sahara Desert was Bilad al-Sudan, land of the blacks, which in practice gradually came to mean the southern part of the Sudan, inhabited by Nilotic and negroid peoples. In this narrative the terms 'the south' and 'southern Sudan' can be taken to mean these three provinces only, while the expressions 'the north' and 'northern Sudan' are applied to the remainder of the country.

The largest country in Africa, the Sudan has an area of about 976,750 square miles; it extends roughly 1,300 miles from north to south and about 950 miles from east to west. Its northern boundary generally follows the 22nd parallel, while on the east it is bounded by the Red Sea and Ethiopia; on the south by Kenya, Uganda and Zaire (formerly the Belgian Congo); and on the west by the Central African Republic and Chad, both formerly French colonial territory, and Libya. The northern and north-eastern regions are mainly arid desert and scrub hills, while the south consists largely of swamp and rain forest, but there are exceptions such as stretches of torrid bush and sun-baked savannah, the huge grassy plains in Bahr el-Ghazal and fertile land in the Gezira. There are four groups of mountains: the Red Sea Hills in Kassala province, the Jebel Marra Range in Darfur province, the Nuba Mountains in Kordofan province, and

[1] For clarity and convenience, present-day names of states and provinces (whose designations may have changed from time to time), will be used throughout to indicate the territory they now encompass.

16

the Immatong and Dongatona Mountains in Equatoria province, the latter two forming the border with Uganda. The highest mountain in the Sudan is Mount Kinyeti, 10,456 feet, in the Immatong range.

The Sudan is dominated and irrigated by the White Nile, the longest river in the world, which enters the country in the south from Uganda at the frontier post of Nimule, in Equatoria province, and flows northwards to enter Egypt near Wadi Halfa. The Blue Nile comes into the Sudan from Ethiopia, and flows about 500 miles to merge with the White Nile at Khartoum. Five of the Nile's six cataracts are between Khartoum and Wadi Halfa; these have formed barriers to navigation from ancient times, as did the Sudd (Arabic for barrier), many miles to the south. At Bor the White Nile over-flows its banks and its surplus waters broaden out to form a huge, 3,000-square mile swamp, choked with reeds and papyrus; apart from the occasional island of firm ground, all else is drifting vegetation and soft mud. There are three main channels through the Sudd, any or all of which may be blocked at times, dependent upon the state of the flood water and drifting vegetation. One is known as the River of Giraffes, another—the main channel usually used by traders in the nineteenth century—is the Bahr el-Jebel, and the third is a long strip of open water known as Lake No. The Sudd terminates at the end of Lake No, and parts of it dry up between November and March, when nomadic Dinkas move in to graze their cattle.

Generally the people of the northern, and larger, part of the Sudan are Hamito-Semites, who like to think of themselves as Arabs; descendants of successive waves of Arab migrations, they probably went first into Egypt and then drifted southwards to settle and inter-marry with the original inhabitants, the Nubians, who were darker and often negroid. Nubia is the ancient name for northern Sudan, the Nubians being the peoples 'living near the Nile', who indeed themselves may have been ancient immigrants. These people are Arabic-speaking, have an Islamic culture and traditionally look north-wards to Egypt and eastwards to Mecca. To the south of a line that vaguely follows the 12th parallel, the inhabitants are negroid and Nilotic, are African in features, outlook and culture, and have close links across the borders of adjoining states, the frontiers of which were arbitrarily drawn by Europeans. There has been only one census in the Sudan, in 1956, when the population was given as being 10,252,536 (2,783,136 in the south and 7,469,400 in the north), some 70 per

17

cent being Arabized northerners and 30 per cent primitive, tribal southerners. The three southern provinces of Bahr el-Ghazal, Upper Nile and Equatoria, which encompass a total of about 250,000 square miles, each have about one million inhabitants. Today the population of the Sudan is estimated to be about 16 million, and so probably in the decades before 1956 it must have been correspondingly less. No one knows exactly.

The people of the south are grouped into three ethnic categories—Nilotic, Nilo-Hamitic and Sudanic.[1] The 1956 census of the whole country recorded 572 different tribes and about 114 languages, of which about 50 of the latter were in the south. The Nilotic category includes the Dinka, the largest group of tribes, estimated to be over one million strong, sub-divided into smaller tribes such as the Cic, Aliah, Bor, Agar and Atot, the Nuer (notable to Europeans because they tend to stand on one leg for long periods like storks), the Shilluk and the Anuak. Each of these groups consists of several tribes, and they live mostly in the Bahr el-Ghazal and Upper Nile provinces, being either agriculturalists or pastoral, depending upon the local terrain. The majority of the Anuak, for example, live over the border in Ethiopia. The Nilo-Hamitic category includes the Murle, Didinga, Boya, Toposa and Latuka, who mainly live in Equatoria province, but bulge over the borders into Uganda and Kenya, while the Sudanic category includes small and numerous tribes living in the western and south-western parts of the south, the most important of which is the Azande. Some of these tribes have not always lived in the south, many having arrived in ancient migrations from the south, east and west. There are other tribes which have developed from fusions of the three main groups, such as the Bari, Mandari, Nyangwara, Faluju, Moru and Luluba. Little is known of the history of the south prior to the nineteenth century, but it is suspected it was a long, confused one of tribal warfare and squabbling. One authority[2] states that 'there may well be tribes isolated in the forests which have never had contact with the outside world'.

The Sudan as such had no political entity in history, and prior to the nineteenth century had no fixed borders either. In ancient times, it is thought, the Kingdom of Kush occupied the area on either side of the River Nile between Khartoum and Wadi Halfa for about a thousand years, until it was eclipsed in the third century A.D. Then

[1] According to *The Southern Sudan* by Mohamed Omer Beshir.
[2] According to *Democracy on Trial* by Mohammed Ahmed Mahgoub.

followed two centuries of which little is known, after which at least three Christian kingdoms arose; in turn these were submerged by Arab invaders in later centuries and converted to Islam.

To the north, Egypt was brought into the Ottoman Empire in 1517, when Cairo was annexed. Over the years it proved to be a restive province, being governed by the Mamelukes, a slave dynasty, who gave nominal allegiance to the Sultan in Constantinople. In 1798 Napoleon Bonaparte, with imperialist aims for republican France, landed in Egypt with an army to defeat a force the Sultan mustered against him at the Battle of Aboukir, after which he fought his way to Cairo, defeating the Mamelukes, practically the only military body available in Egypt. Napoleon entered Cairo and dominated Egypt, and there was little the Sultan could do about it. Lord Nelson defeated the French fleet at the Battle of the Nile in 1798, and in the following year Napoleon secretly abandoned his army and returned to France. Alarmed by this French intrusion on the route to India, the British landed a small expeditionary force in Egypt, which scattered the remnants of the French army left behind by Napoleon. Then both British and French troops withdrew (in 1801 and 1802), leaving chaos behind in Egypt, out of which Mohammed Ali rose to prominence.

Born at Kavalla in Greece, then part of the Ottoman Empire, Mohammed Ali was a soldier of fortune who had landed with an Albanian detachment to take part in the disastrous Battle of Aboukir, when he, with others, was pushed into the sea by the British, being rescued, it is sometimes said, by British sailors. He made himself leader of the Albanian detachment, which was about 10,000 strong, and then began to struggle successfully for political power against the Mamelukes and others. He was proclaimed Pasha of Egypt in 1805. In 1811 he treacherously slaughtered the majority of the Mamelukes, and so removed his major threat. Next he became involved in a war in Arabia that dragged on for seven years, to end with his brief occupation of Mecca. Later, in 1841, he was created Khedive, hereditary ruler, of Egypt by the Sultan.[1] Having defeated and scattered the Mamelukes, the caste of fighting soldiers, Mohammed Ali decided to build a new model army of freed slaves and slaves, to make himself independent of Arab and other factions. Short of money after his Arabian adventure, he turned his eyes southwards towards the Bilad al-Sudan, the still unknown land from whence came

[1] A firman from the Sultan was dated the 1st June 1841.

slaves, and which was also rumoured to contain gold and ivory in plenty.

Along the River Nile in northern Sudan there were a number of small independent rulers, of varying strength, power and influence, and also others in more remote parts of the country, who had never before been brought under central authority. Commencing in 1821, Mohammed Ali sent armies, notably two commanded by two of his sons, southwards to conquer and obtain slaves in great number, and to search for the mythical riches. In 1824, after subduing the once-powerful Funj Kingdom of Sennar, he established and fortified a military post at Khartoum[1] at the junction of the White and Blue Niles, and a string of other small military posts began to radiate out from it and along the White Nile. Mohammed Ali made only one visit to the Sudan himself, of four months' duration, in 1830, but when he died in 1841 he had annexed, although not pacified, Dongola province, Berber (the region between the first and third cataracts), Sennar (an important trans-African market), Kordofan province and the Suakin coastal region. By 1852 the southern limit of Egyptian influence had reached Aba Island, about 250 miles south of Khartoum, in the White Nile. This period, from 1821 to 1884, was known as the Turkia, because the inhabitants thought the invaders to be Turks, although few were of that nationality.

Slavery had been customary in the Sudan from time immemorial, the slaves being either captured in war, taken on slave raids or bought in the various slave markets, such as that at Sennar, but prior to the nineteenth century it had probably been on a much smaller scale than is generally believed, the slaves being mainly obtained for domestic work or to labour in the fields. Mohammed Ali began the advent of mass slave-taking, his administration in the Sudan being specially geared for this purpose. It has been estimated[2] that during the nineteenth century, Arab slavers carried off about 'two million blacks' from the southern Sudan. Failing to find the fabled riches of Bilad al-Sudan, Mohammed Ali had to rely upon the slave trade to provide him with wealth. The legendary gold mines at Falughli, on the Ethiopian border, were already worked out and there was little evidence they had ever been very productive, while the trade in ivory tusks was so small that it did not contribute anything materially to the regime's coffers.

[1] Means 'elephant's trunk', or 'snout', which it was thought to resemble in shape.
[2] According to *Sudan: the Long War*, Institute for the Study of Conflict pamphlet, March 1972.

The revulsion towards slavery that mounted in the western world began to influence the Sultan at Constantinople, who in 1847 nominally forbade slave-trading in his empire. He was echoed by Khedive Said, of Egypt, in 1860. But to eradicate slavery was far easier decreed than done. Slavery continued to be rife, especially in the Sudan, where it had become big business, and when restrictions on movement into the Sudan from Egypt were lifted in 1853, slave-traders moved rapidly southwards ahead of the more slowly penetrating Khedival authority. The possession of fire-arms enabled them to dominate the inhabitants, and some slave-traders became powerful merchant-brigands, with their own private armies of enlisted slaves securely ensconced in forts, who made private agreements with local chiefs. The decade, 1869–79, was one in which the tough struggle took place between the Egyptian Government, which employed foreign soldiers and administrators, including some European, and the slavers.

A Turkish naval captain, dispatched by Mohammed Ali to sail up the White Nile from Khartoum, set off in 1839, and by the following year he had forced a passage through the Sudd as far as Bor. He then moved up river to Rejaf, a total journey of over 1,000 miles, and by early 1841 had reached Gondokoro. He had really opened up the route south along the river for the first time in history, and so paved the way for the second phase of opening up the south, which was begun by Khedive Ismail in 1863. Ismail had been educated in France and was influenced by European ideas. Within fifteen years he had, nominally at least, added the southern Sudan to his domain, commencing with the Fashoda[1] area. Other regions were gained by setting the merchant brigands against each other, and in 1873 Bahr el-Ghazal was won over by making one of them its Governor and recognizing him as such. The Suez Canal was opened in 1869, and soon became a busy route to India and the Far East, attracting increasing European interest. Khedive Ismail, who was falling heavily into European debt, was persuaded to make further efforts to suppress the slave trade in the Sudan. He agreed, mainly because he wanted to recruit the Egyptian fellaheen into his new army, instead of Negroes who were, or had been, slaves. The opening of the Sudd had cleared the way for the slave-traders into the south.

In 1869 the Khedive employed Sir Samuel Baker, an Englishman, to lead an expedition into the south, with orders to establish a chain of forts and to suppress slave trading. It was Baker who took the

---

[1] Renamed the Upper Nile province in 1902.

Egyptian flag to the Uganda frontier, and organized Egyptian garrisons in the south along the White Nile, but he had little success against the slave-traders, many of whom were secure in their forts away from the river, or off the main trade route. Slavery was too old a custom to be eradicated overnight by a handful of soldiers. In 1877 Khedive Ismail signed a Slave Trade Convention, agreeing that all such trade in his domain should cease by 1889—but he was deposed in 1879, mainly for his financial shortcomings.

In 1874 Baker was succeeded by General Gordon, who had achieved a brilliant but unconventional military reputation in China. Egyptian nominal control was gained over Darfur province when its Sultan was killed in battle. The telegraph line, which had reached Khartoum, stretched out to El Obeid and to the borders of Darfur, while to the east it reached the Red Sea at Suakin. Given the title of Governor of Equatoria province,[1] General Gordon established a provincial capital at Lado, organized more garrisons and improved the chain of forts along the river, but when he left in 1876 Egyptian authority was still tenuous and the slave trade continued to flourish. After a short break Gordon was appointed Governor-General of the Sudan, charged with pacifying the country and suppressing the slave trade. He had some initial success in preventing slaves being carried northwards along the Nile by employing on this task the small body of river police that had been formed in 1864, but bribery and corruption generally nullified his efforts in this respect.

The next period of history in the Sudan, known as the Mahdia, lasted from 1881 until 1898. In 1881 Mohammed Ahmed ibn Abdullah, a native of the Dongola area, wrote, from where he was staying on Aba Island, to many chiefs and notables in the Sudan, claiming to be the expected 'Mahdi',[2] or Messiah, and calling upon them to rise and unite behind him. Thus began the Mahdi Revolt, and Mohammed Ahmed's followers, who soon numbered several thousands, became known as the Ansar.[3] The main cause of the revolt was the general hatred of the Egyptians, whose 28,000 troops garrisoning the Sudan behaved badly and in an overbearing manner to the Sudanese.

This was the first sign of nationalism, or even cohesion, in the Sudan, and the Mahdi has been referred to by latter-day nationalists

[1] Then known as Mongalla.
[2] According to Mahgoub—Mahdi means 'Guided One' or 'Expected Guide'.
[3] The original Ansar were the 'Helpers' of the Prophet Mohammed at Medina.

as Abu al-Istiqal, the Father of Independence. He was also the first to bring the diverse Muslim tribes together to fight against a foreign invader. In 1882 he surrounded El Obeid with a force of about 30,000 Ansar, many of whom had formerly served in the Egyptian army, and starved the town into submission. General Hicks, with a small army of about 8,000 soldiers, who had cleared the Mahdists out from the Gezira, was told to retake El Obeid, but the Ansar filled in the water holes along his route, and 50,000 of them surrounded him at Rahad, keeping the men awake all night by beating on tins. The Ansar finally attacked Hicks's thirsty and weary force at Shaikan, near El Obeid, and annihilated it completely. During the next few months the Mahdi seized Darfur province, taking prisoner the Austrian Governor, Slatin. So far the Mahdi Revolt had embraced only the Islamic tribes, and although the Mahdi gained control over Bahr el-Ghazal province in 1884, he recalled his Ansar from that area. Then, after some fighting against the Ethiopians, he began marching northwards on to Khartoum.

The British Government, briefly non-imperialistic in foreign policy, decided to persuade the Egyptians to evacuate the Sudan, and General Gordon, who was recalled to prominence by a British press campaign, was sent out to conduct the withdrawal back into Egypt. Reappointed Governor-General, he arrived at Khartoum on the 18th February 1884. The telegraph line was cut on the 17th March, he was soon besieged by Ansar, and the Mahdi himself arrived outside the city on the 23rd October. Meanwhile the British Government had changed its mind, and a military force was mustered in Egypt to relieve Khartoum. On the 26th January 1885 the Mahdi's forces attacked the city, Gordon was killed,[1] and Khartoum was sacked. The river steamers, carrying troops of the relief force, arrived on the 28th—three days too late, and had to turn back.

Mohammed Ahmed died on the 22nd June 1885, and was succeeded as Mahdi by Khailifa Abdullah, one of his followers, who continued the holy war. Although he brought most of the Sudan under his sway, he had to fight continually to maintain his authority. In 1888 he launched a second Mahdi invasion into the south, but his attempts to conquer Equatoria province were resisted by the local

[1] According to Mahgoub, whose grandfather was an Ansar commander at this battle, the Mahdi had given orders that Gordon was not to be killed, but one over-enthusiastic Ansar disobeyed them. The Mahdi held an enquiry, but was not able to find the culprit.

tribes, remnants of the Egyptian army and the Belgians from the adjacent Congo. Wherever possible the Mahdi attempted to force the Islamic religion on the southerners, which caused hostility, and he also legalized slavery. Throughout, whenever they could, the Negro tribes of the south fought hard against the Ansar, who were finally compelled to withdraw in 1897, when the Belgians established their authority in the Lado Enclave. On the 3rd August 1889 the defeat of the Mahdi's forces at the Battle of Tuski, a few miles north of Wadi Halfa, eliminated the Mahdist threat to Egypt. The Ansar then became involved in fighting the Ethiopians as well as having to cope with a rebellion in Darfur, Kordofan and along the White Nile.

In 1882, when Colonel Ahmed Arabi led a military revolt in Egypt, a British expedition under General Sir Garnet Wolseley was sent to restore the authority of the Khedive, and Arabi and his rebellious Egyptian troops were scattered at the Battle of Tel el-Kebir, on the 13th September 1882. Reinstated, the Khedive surrendered more power to the British, sank deeper into financial difficulties, and his country virtually became a British protectorate. The 'mad scramble for Africa' was at its height, and under British initiative, but nominally in the Khedive's name, the reconquest of the Sudan was begun in 1896. After a series of engagements the main forces of the Mahdi were brought to battle near Omdurman, on the 1st September 1898, by an Anglo-Egyptian army, supported by ten river gunboats which bombarded the city. The following day the Mahdi launched his 60,000 primitively armed Ansar into battle. The result was that 10,563 of them were killed and another 16,000 wounded, for the Allied loss of only 49 dead and 382 wounded. The temporal power of the Mahdi was broken by modern fire-power. The Mahdi escaped from the field at Omdurman, but was later run to earth and killed in a clash near Kaka, on the River Nile, some 300 miles south of Aba Island, on the 23rd November 1899.

The scramble for Africa continued as British, Italians, French and Belgians rushed in to grasp what pieces of territory remained unclaimed by any European nation. Considering the Sudan since the Mahdi Revolt to be unclaimed, the French decided to try to seize it; they sent two forces, one from Central Africa and the other from the Red Sea. Even before the Battle of Omdurman had been fought a small French party, under Captain Jean-Baptiste Marchand, which had left Brazzaville, in the Congo, in 1896, made an amazing 3,000-mile march across Africa to arrive at Fashoda (now Kodok), the centre of the priest-kings of the Shilluk, early in July 1898. To forestall British reoccupation, Marchand claimed the Upper Nile for France. He had been instructed to contact the Emperor Menelik, of Ethiopia, and to come to an agreement with him over this. The other French expedition from the Red Sea had arrived earlier but, seeing no sign of Marchand, had returned to the coast again. This French claim caused international repercussions, but was finally settled by diplomatic means, the French eventually withdrawing.

The British, who virtually ruled Egypt and certainly dictated its foreign policy, had supported the Egyptian claim to the Sudan, but they were reluctant to restore Egyptian authority, which they desired for themselves, so they came up with the plan for a condominium that provided for joint British and Egyptian rule. The Condominium Agreement was signed on the 19th January 1899, but power was seized and wielded by the British, hardly any being given to the Egyptians.

So far the only fixed boundary of the Sudan was its northern one, but gradually its frontiers were delineated by a series of agreements. After the French withdrawal from Fashoda in 1899, the Belgians renewed their claim to parts of the south, including the Lado Enclave, which they had occupied since the Mahdi Revolt and which was granted to King Leopold II for life. On his death, in 1909, they reverted to the Condominium and the frontier was demarcated. In 1902, under British pressure, to prevent splitting two natural regions, Egypt agreed to transfer to the Sudan a 90-square-mile piece of land in the Nile Valley near Wadi Halfa, and a 6,700-square-mile triangle of desert and scrub hills around Haliab on the Red Sea coast.[1] Frontier agreements with Ethiopia and Uganda were concluded in 1913.

Apart from the extreme dislike of the Egyptian soldiery, bad administration, heavy taxation and efforts to suppress the slave trade had contributed towards the Mahdi Revolt. These problems remained to be dealt with in a Sudan that was lawless and seething with discontent. The first essential was pacification, a task that took several years. By December 1899 the railhead had reached the Blue Nile opposite Khartoum, and in 1903 a much larger channel was forced through the Sudd, which facilitated navigation. The country was divided into six provinces, each governed by a military officer with considerable powers, on the principle of 'indirect rule', that is,

[1] In 1958 President Nasser of Egypt demanded their return.

25

ruling through the local chiefs, who were often placed in office, and supported by the Governor. The British made the office of chief hereditary, which tended to cause discontent. Tribal insurrection was frequent; for example, expeditions had to be dispatched against the Atwok Dinka in 1907,[1] against the Beir in 1908, and against the Twig Dinka in 1911. In 1912 the Anuak killed 47 soldiers, including 5 officers, and in 1914 another military expedition had to be sent against them. In 1919 the Aliab Dinka killed the Governor of Bahr el-Ghazal province. In all, five expeditions had to be sent against them, the last in 1923. At least another nine were sent against the Nuer, who lived on the east bank of the White Nile in Upper Nile province, who had killed their District Commissioner in 1927.[2] The last was sent in 1928. It was not until 1930 that the Administration was confident enough to assert that the Sudan was pacified. Even so, rumbles of insurrection and violent tribal squabbles continued. As recently as 1941 a District Commissioner was severely wounded in a spear attack.

There was also continuing friction along the unruly border with Ethiopia. Between 1916 and 1927, for example, there were 41 Ethiopian incursions into the Kassala and Upper Nile provinces, and 23 into Mongalla,[3] in addition to organized slave-raiding and arms-running all along the frontier.[4]

Slavery declined with the progress of pacification. The decline was slow, however, despite Lord Kitchener's optimistic statement in 1912, that 'Slave trading on a large scale is clearly a thing of the past.' It lingered on mainly in the regions adjoining Ethiopia. In fact, a flourishing slave-trade route across the Upper White Nile was discovered as late as 1929. Although a former slave was legally free to leave his master, he was usually enchained by economic circumstances, and large numbers of technically freed slaves, or descendants of slaves, worked as unpaid servants or labourers for their old masters because they had nowhere to go and no means of earning money to buy food.

Despite the usual hard line taken by Islam against Christian missionaries generally, Mohammed Ali and his successors were comparatively lenient towards them, and a few had been allowed to enter the Sudan from the north. Commencing in 1845, Roman Catholics

[1] According to Beshir.
[2] According to *The Southern Sudan* by Dunstan M Wai.
[3] In 1937, Mongalla merged with Bahr el-Ghazal to become Equatoria province, but Bahr el-Ghazal again became a separate province in 1945.
[4] According to *The Sudan* by MacMichael.

began to obtain footholds. They established mission stations, one of the first being at Gondokoro in 1850, and another at Kaka in 1862. These were followed by a mission school in Khartoum. Wishing to end the preponderance of Roman Catholics, in 1871 General Gordon, when Governor of Equatoria, wrote to the Church Missionary Society in England inviting it to send out missionaries, and a few arrived. However, all Christian missions and schools were eliminated by the zeal of the Ansar in the areas affected by the Mahdi Revolt.

When the power of the Mahdi was broken European and American missionary societies wanted to move into the Sudan, especially into the open south, to convert the inhabitants to Christianity. At first, surprisingly, they met resistance from the British authorities on the ground, who were reluctant to let them in because they would 'spoil the natives', although they were against the spread of Islamic influence into the south. Pressure from within Britain caused this decision to be overruled by the British Government. It was agreed that missionaries might establish churches and schools in the Muslim parts of the Sudan, but must not proselytize; to the south of the 10th parallel, that is in the south with the exception of an area in the north-east of Bahr el-Ghazal province, they had freedom of action. The south was parcelled out to the various religious orders and denominations, a system that was not popular amongst the Roman Catholic orders, which thought they should have more territory and be allowed to expand.

The Roman Catholic Italian Verona Fathers established schools at Detwok and Lul, in Upper Nile province, in 1901; the American Presbyterian Mission started work at Doleib Hill, also in Upper Nile province, in 1902; the Church Missionary Society established a school at Bor in 1905, another at Malek in 1906, and yet another at Yei in 1917; and the Sudan United Mission opened small boarding schools at Rom and Pachola, and then a co-educational one at Melut in 1913. Both the Anglican (Anglicans were known as Episcopalians in the Sudan) Missionary Society and the American United Mission were at work in the south by 1905, and were joined in 1913 by the Australian and New Zealand United Mission. The Austrian Carmelite Friars, who had also established themselves in the south, were ejected in 1914, when World War I broke out, and their places were taken, after 1918, by the Verona Fathers. By 1914 there were Anglican, Greek Orthodox and Coptic cathedrals in Khartoum, and churches in many other towns.

27

The missionaries taught in English or the local language, and teachers were brought in from Uganda missions and elsewhere to help, but there was a lack of a common educational policy among the missions themselves, hardly any liaison or co-operation, and no guidance from the Government. In 1918 English became the official language of the south, and Sunday became the weekly day of rest, instead of the Muslim Friday. Some doubted the wisdom of entrusting education to the missionaries in the south, especially as the pupil had to accept Christianity before he was educated, which automatically debarred the few Muslims, the mass of animists and anyone who could not accept Christian beliefs and doctrines, but as money and facilities were unavailable, there seemed to be little option. Eventually in 1926 the mission schools were subsidized by the Government; the theory was that they should give education to all regardless of religion, but in practice the southerner had to become a Christian to gain an education at all. In the north there were some Government schools as well as the many Ulema (religious) ones, where all instruction was in Arabic, and in general literacy, other than in the labouring or nomadic classes in the Arab world was far higher than is usually supposed. In 1902 the Gordon Memorial College was opened in Khartoum, which gave a form of higher education, in English.

The British administrators looked in doubt at the three southern provinces, so utterly unlike those in the north. There were at times whispers, even mutterings, that it would be better to sever them from the Sudan and move them into the African ethnic block, attaching them either to Kenya or Uganda, when a large nominally Christian Negro belt could stand as a barrier against the Muslim north. They were convinced that Islam should be prevented from permeating the south. In 1902 the decision was made to treat the south separately from the north, and to consider them as two entities in different stages of development and progress. In 1922 the south was formally declared to be a 'closed district' and Muslim traders and others were practically debarred from entry to many parts of it, while the Permits to Trade Order, of 1925, further controlled entry into, and trading in, the south. The British officials declared that these measures were aimed at protecting the southerners from northern exploitation.

In November 1914, when Turkey entered World War I on the side of Germany, Britain declared a Protectorate over Egypt, and the Khedive was deposed. There was little trouble in general in the Muslim north during the war, except in Darfur province, where the

Sultan declared his loyalty to the Ottoman Empire and in May 1915 called upon the sheikhs in adjacent Kordofan province to rise with him in revolt against the British. It was not until May 1916 that a military force could be assembled to march against the rebellious Sultan of Darfur, who was killed in battle, after which the revolt subsided and the affected areas again came under central control. There was no trouble in this respect in the south during World War I, despite the initial presence of Austrian missionaries, who were soon interned. The boundary between the Sudan and French Equatorial Africa was delineated in 1919.

After the war, on the 22nd February 1922, the British Protectorate over Egypt ended. The country became independent and Ahmed Fuad was proclaimed King. The Condominium remained in force, but became a source of friction between Britain and Egypt, while considerable unease arose in the Sudan as the politically conscious Egyptians, imbued with new national pride, tried to elbow the British administrators aside. Early projects in the Sudan had been financed by the Egyptians, who had also made up the annual deficit in the Sudanese budget until it finally balanced in 1913 for the first time. The more nationalist-minded Egyptians began to agitate for a greater share in the administration of the Condominium, which was resisted by the British.

The Egyptians sought to subvert the Sudanese and turn them against the British. On the 9th August 1924 cadets at the Military School at Khartoum made an armed demonstration through the streets, which coincided with a mutiny of the Egyptian Railway Battalion at Atbara, where the soldiers ran amock for three days. Support for the cadet demonstration and the mutiny was given by an element of the 'freed slaves' and their descendants in the north who, together with the Nuba tribesmen, formed the majority at the Military School, and indeed in the Egyptian battalions in the Sudan. There were also disorders at Port Sudan and Malakal at the same time.

On the 19th November 1924 Sir Lee Stack, Governor-General of Egypt and Commander-in-Chief (Sirdar) of its armed forces, was assassinated in a Cairo street. The British Government took immediate strong action. All Egyptian officers and soldiers in the Sudan were ordered to withdraw into Egypt within twenty-four hours, and British troops surrounded Egyptian units in and around Khartoum. Most left with extreme reluctance. For example, one Egyptian battalion was forcibly entrained at Khartoum under the barrels of

British machine-guns, and another was evacuated in a similar manner. Before it left, however, the latter unit had managed to spread discontent within the Sudanese units of the Khartoum garrison. On the 27th November two platoons, with six Sudanese officers, of the 11th Sudanese Battalion mutinied, and when they refused to obey orders British soldiers opened fire on them. The mutineers assaulted the Military Hospital at Khartoum, killing one British and two Syrian medical officers and one British and three Egyptian soldiers. The building was surrounded and bombarded by artillery fire until the 29th, when the mutiny was quelled. Other Egyptian resistance collapsed and the remaining Egyptian personnel were quickly evacuated.

Less than 200 Sudanese soldiers were involved in the mutiny. Some of them surrendered; some escaped into the city, causing trouble before they were disarmed and arrested; others fled into the countryside; others were concealed by friends; and yet others made good their escape into Egypt. Of the six Sudanese officers, one who turned state evidence was sentenced to imprisonment, one was killed in the fighting, another was wounded but succeeded in escaping with the evacuating Egyptians, and the other three were eventually executed. The Military School was closed and the new Sudan Defence Force was formed. All Egyptian officials and teachers were also ejected, and so ended the first real Egyptian attempt to assert their rule over the Sudan.

In 1930 the British administrators redefined their southern policy of separating the north from the south. It had in fact begun in 1902, and been furthered in 1922, because they feared that the newly emerging anti-British sentiments in the north, encouraged by Egyptian factions, might spread into the south, and from there into British East African territory. On the 25th January it was decreed that the object was to 'build up a series of self-contained racial and tribal units with structure and organization based, to whatever extent the requirements of equity and good government permit, upon indigenous customs, traditional usages and beliefs'.[1] The principle of indirect rule was clearly restated. The use of Arabic was discouraged and that of English encouraged, and an even stricter control was exercised over Muslims entering the south. Until 1934 it was thought that the south contained more than half the population of the Sudan.

[1] According to *The War in the Sudan*, by Cecil Eprile.

A brief comment must be made about efforts to improve the administration and economy of the Sudan at this stage. The small group of British administrators and officials remained in the country for their whole careers (unlike British Foreign and Colonial Office personnel who rotated from country to country), and upon retiring left the Sudan and did not settle there. Nevertheless, well paid and of very high quality as they were, they came to identify themselves closely with the country they served and its people, and it became their intention to make the Sudan independent of Egypt and economically self-sufficient. As a first step they had recruited and trained a body of clerks, but these were practically all northerners. Next, they began to develop a cadre of junior administrators, who were also predominantly northerners, owing to their educational advantages.

As none of the legendary gold, or any other minerals in commercial quantities, had been discovered, and the only export of note was gum arabic, of which the Sudan then supplied 90 per cent of the world's output, it was decided to grow cotton as a staple crop, and in 1925 the Gezira Scheme was launched. The Gezira was the area of fertile land between the White and Blue Niles, which could be easily irrigated. By 1952 the original 300,000 acres had increased to 1 million, despite setbacks due to cotton disease and to the world depression of 1929–31. Practically all economic projects, such as the construction of roads, railways and bridges, agricultural experiments and irrigation schemes, were confined to the Muslim north, while the south, in this respect almost completely overlooked and ignored, remained undeveloped.

The conquest of Ethiopia by the Italians, which commenced in 1935, altered the balance of power in Africa, and the Egyptians became restless at the continuing presence of British troops in their capital. The Anglo-Egyptian Treaty, by which the British agreed to remove their troops from Cairo into the Suez Canal Zone, was signed on the 26th August 1936, but the Condominium, still administered by a British Governor-General on behalf of both countries, remained, although the Egyptian part was almost a fiction.

2 Mutiny of the Equatoria Corps: 1955

'Allah wept when he created the Sudan.'

Another Arab proverb

Political awakening was slow in the Sudan. After the eclipse of the Mahdia, Sudanese nationalism lay dormant until, in 1921, Ali Abdul Latif, a Dinka officer, founded the Sudanese United Tribes Society, which called for independence, but he was imprisoned the following year. In May 1924, after his release from prison, he founded the White Flag League, which called for unity of the Nile Valley, and he stated his willingness to work with the Egyptians to expel the British. He led an army mutiny, which was quelled by British troops with some loss of life, after which he was again imprisoned and his organizations faded out. Political activity did not manifest itself again until February 1938, when a more stable political organization appeared, the Graduates General Congress, whose members were drawn from those with a secondary education and included a large proportion of government officials. Its secretary, Ismail al-Azhari, was cautious and his demands mild. Although it was pointed out that the Congress represented only a very tiny fraction of the people, an alliance grew between it and the two rival religious sects, the Ansar and the Khatmia, both of which commanded a considerable following. The Khatmia, favouring the Ottoman sultans, had been harshly treated by the Ansar during the Mahdi Revolt, and so mutual antagonism had developed, heightened when the Ansar supported the British during World War I, which the Khatmia did not. One other organization appeared during 1938, and that was the Black Bloc, ostensibly a social organization, but its political branch was quickly suppressed because of its anti-Arab character, the members being drawn from Negro groups in the north.

Influenced by the world-wide wave of independence and nationalism sweeping through colonized territories, on the 3rd April 1942

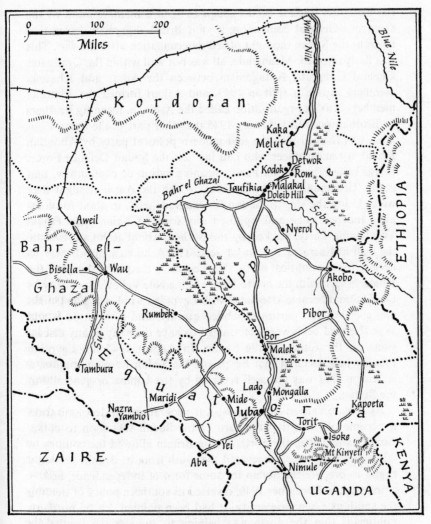

The Southern Sudan

B

the Congress became bold enough to send a memorandum to the Governor-General demanding a joint British–Egyptian declaration to grant the Sudan the right of self-determination after the war. This was flatly rejected. Meanwhile, all was not well within the Graduates General Congress. Antagonism between the Ansar and Khatmia members caused a split in 1943, and Azhari formed the Khatmia members into an organization called the Ashikka, meaning Brothers or Brotherhood. In February 1945 the other part of the dying Congress was formed into the first modern political party by Abdullah Khalil, a senior officer who had just left the Sudan Defence Force. It was called the Umma Party, meaning nation or community, that is the 'Community of the Faithful', which the Ansar thought they were. Using the slogan 'Sudan for the Sudanese', it stood for complete independence and opposed any form of union with Egypt. The Umma Party, backed by the Mahdi, Abdul Rahman, became the political arm of the Ansar sect. The Ashikka's riposte was to declare itself a political party, thus becoming the political arm of the Khatmia sect, with the motto 'Unity of the Nile Valley'. Accordingly, the Khatmia became associated with Egypt in its policies. The Umma and the Ashikka parties expanded quickly, and as soon as World War II ended both were determined to have their say in any discussions on the future of the Sudan. In August 1944 the Egyptian Premier had declared that Egypt and the Sudan were one nation, a statement that was not well received by the Umma or generally in the Sudan.

As Britain carried out its post-war programme of decolonization it became obvious that the turn of the Sudan was soon to come. Anxiety was felt in the north in case Britain allowed the country to fall to the Egyptians, or severed the south from it. Britain belatedly began to prepare the Sudan for some form of independence, and as a first step, in December 1946, reversed its southern policy of treating the south as a separate entity. It had been pointed out by northern politicians that the north was helping to support the south; for example, in 1947 the north was about to pay nearly one million pounds to make up the deficit in southern revenue.

To promote this fusion, the Juba Conference, attended by numbers of southern chiefs, educated southerners, a few northerners and some British officials, was held on the 12th and 13th June 1947. Part of the object of the conference was to gauge the views of southerners, which had never been really put forward before, but this was overshadowed by northern insistence on unity, which was backed by the British. It was laid down that Arabic was to be the official language; this meant that mission schools, which since 1927 had almost complete control over southern education, had to change their medium of teaching and curriculum. The pace of Sudanization began to quicken, and as British officials left the country they were replaced by Sudanese, who were practically all northerners. The reason given was that southerners generally were debarred from senior government posts by lack of education and by not being able to speak and read Arabic.[1] The small English-speaking intelligentzia, if that expression can be used, created by the missionaries, which now had to learn Arabic to be eligible for the senior posts, felt it was being unfairly excluded. The Juba Conference was the first time that southerners had come together to discuss their political future.

During 1948 elections were held for a National Assembly,[2] but the Ashikka boycotted them. There were disturbances in Omdurman, and Azhari was arrested. Concurrently with political development the trade union movement grew in the Sudan; there had been a railway workers' strike in the previous year. The National Assembly was formally opened on the 15th December 1948, and consisted of 75 elected members and a small number of nominated ones; of these, 76 were northerners and only 13 were southerners. An executive council was formed to govern the country in what was to be an interim period. More political parties began to appear, but all were northern in composition and aims. In August 1949 the National Front was formed, which stood for dominion status under Egyptian suzerainty, but in 1952 it faded out. In March 1951 an Anglo-Sudanese Constitution Amendment Commission was established to advise the Governor-General on the stages to be taken to grant self-government to the Sudan.

In 1951 the Ashikka Party split into two parts over the issue of independence or some form of association with Egypt, but by Egyptian intervention the rift was healed. With the two parts reunited, the party was renamed the National Unionist Party (NUP) and was still led by Azhari. In December of that year yet another

[1] According to *The Sudan*, by Oliver Albino, it was not until 1942 that the first southerners were allowed to sit for the civil service examination; only 1 southerner was selected for a post in 1944, 2 in 1946 and 12 in 1948.

[2] This expression is used throughout for convenience and clarity as this body had various names at different times, such as Legislative Assembly, Constituent Assembly and People's Assembly.

35

political party was formed, the Socialist Republican Party, composed of 'tribal notables' and personalities who had gained prominence in the 'native administration' under the British. This new party gained support from members of the Assembly, and was opposed to Azhari's pro-Egyptian line. These political parties now began to speak of a Sudanese nation, a term that had formerly only been applied to the south, and they claimed to speak for all the Sudanese, both northerners and southerners.

In 1951 King Farouk proclaimed himself King of Egypt and the Sudan, but by this time the idea of an independent Sudan had gripped most Sudanese politicians, even though some, like Azhari, remained pro-Egyptian in sentiment. The Egyptian Government would not agree to changes the British were making in the Sudan unless the authority of the Egyptian crown was recognized, and Britain now came into dispute with Egypt over this and other matters. On the 8th October 1951 the Egyptian Government abrogated the Anglo-Egyptian Treaty of 1936, and also terminated the agreement on the Condominium over the Sudan. King Farouk was toppled from his throne in July 1952 by a military coup, which brought General Neguib to power. In June 1953 the country was declared a republic, and in November 1954 Neguib was deposed by Gamel Abdul Nasser, who eventually became President on the 23rd June 1956. In 1952 the British had made a Self-Determination Agreement with the Sudanese, and on the 12th February 1953 an Anglo-Egyptian Agreement was signed which guaranteed the Sudanese the right to determine their own future. Four Sudanese political parties were present at the conference preceding this event, at which there was no southern representative at all.

An embryo southern political party had in fact been formed in 1951 by Buth Diu (a Nuer), Stanislaus Paysama (a Dinka) and Abdul Rahman Sale (a southern Muslim), but it only had a shadowy form until, disappointed at their non-representation on national issues, and determined that their political voice should be heard in future, many southerners joined Buth Diu's party, which rapidly expanded and in 1953 became known as the Southern Party. Another reason for supporting this party, the only southern one, was that the south would be able to campaign in the forthcoming elections. The Southern Party changed its name to the Liberal Party in 1954, in an attempt to gain northern members, but it was unsuccessful, and so it changed its title again, this time to the Southern Liberal Party.

A little later on it reverted to its original name of the Southern Party. The Black Bloc, although remaining in being, had been ineffective, and it faded out in 1955.

The year 1953 was a vital one as elections were held during November and December. The pro-Egyptian NUP made special efforts to woo the south, while the Egyptian Government almost openly intervened, spending large sums of money and pouring out a steady stream of propaganda over Radio Cairo to try to persuade the Sudanese politicians and people to agree to merge with Egypt. Major Saleh Salem, an Egyptian Government representative, achieved notoriety as the 'dancing major', when he took off his shirt and joined in a Dinka dance, as he cajoled and wheedled the Sudanese at the hustings. As he toured the south he promised the southerners 40 senior government posts when the British left—something he had no authority to do.

The election was won by Azhari's NUP, which gained 51 out of a total of 97 seats. When the new National Assembly met on the 1st January 1954 he formed a government from his NUP members. The Southern Party won only 12 seats out of the south's allocation of 26.[1] On the whole the elections, the first ever, were not properly understood by the illiterate inhabitants of the south, many being suspicious of the whole procedure.

One of Premier Azhari's first acts was to appoint on the 20th February 1954 the Sudanization Committee, which at the end of July reported that there were 800 posts to be Sudanized, so a public service commission was set up to effect recruitment and appointments to these posts. The Sudan was now fully in the transitional period of 'self administration' as the prelude to complete independence. At the end of 1953 there were 140 British officials, 8 senior police officers, and 30 officers serving with the Sudan Defence Force, all of whom left the Sudan during 1954. In this huge phase of Sudanization the southerners obtained only 6 of the 800 posts, the remainder going to northerners.

The Southern Party, with Stanislaus Paysama as its president, and Buth Diu as its secretary-general, called upon all southern members of the National Assembly, regardless of party loyalties, to form the Southern Bloc, which all did; indeed, two members of the NUP switched over to it as well. In October 1954 the Southern Party held

---

[1] Of the southern seats, the Southern Party obtained 12, the NUP 10 and the Independents 4.

37

a conference in Juba, which called unanimously for federal status for the south. Another Southern Party conference was planned for June 1955, also to be held at Juba.

The Sudan Defence Force (SDF) came officially into existence on the 1st January 1925, after the mutiny and troubles of the previous year. When Egyptian officers were ejected it was led solely by seconded British army officers. Its organization was irregular as it had developed to meet varying needs in different parts of this huge country, which was divided into five military regions. There were four 'corps', all dissimilar: the Eastern Arab Corps, based on Kassala, consisting mainly of infantry companies, with a small mounted detachment; the Camel Corps in Kordofan, with a large element of camel-borne soldiers to patrol the vast desert expanses; the Western Arab Corps in Darfur, consisting of a few mounted companies; and the Equatoria[1] Corps in the three southern provinces, consisting of infantry companies—as, even leaving the tsetse fly out of account, camels and horses were of little value in the forest and swamp. Additionally, there was a detachment of cavalry at Shendi and of engineers at Omdurman, the total establishment being just under 5,000.

During the early years of the Condominium, troops in the Sudan had been part of the Egyptian army, which then basically consisted of eight Egyptian (that is, serving in Egypt) and seven Sudanese (serving in the Sudan) battalions; the latter was officered by both British and Egyptians, the soldiers being Egyptian fellaheen and Sudanese. The Sudanese units had been retained and reorganized into the new SDF, with all Egyptian personnel excluded. The main problems were those of immense distances and quarrelling tribes. The SDF had no artillery, but there was a British military presence in the background in the Sudan at Khartoum, Atbara and Port Sudan. Just before World War II the Camel Corps and certain other mounted detachments were mechanized, being given trucks for patrolling, and armed with machine-guns.

The SDF was a territorial force. There was little or no rotation of units; the soldiers bought their own food and lived with their families near their sub-unit HQs. When on patrol they were given an allowance of grain or flour as rations. This completely volunteer force was comparatively well paid according to the norms of the country and the times; the soldiers usually engaged for short-term contracts, but normally they could extend their service, and so a

[1] Often referred to as the Southern Corps.

hard core of long-service warrant and non-commissioned officers was formed. Service in the SDF was extremely popular and had great prestige value, there being no shortage of volunteers to select recruits from when required. Discharged soldiers enjoyed a certain prestige when they returned to their own villages. British personnel held all the senior and key appointments in the SDF, but it was possible (and had been since 1905) for the Sudanese to become junior officers, if they successfully passed the two-year course at the Sudan military college; but again, owing to superior educational opportunities, most of the Sudanese officers were northerners.

While the south was being penetrated and pacified, detachments of the (then) Egyptian army consisted solely of northern soldiers and Egyptians. No thought was given to enlisting southerners until 1910 when the Governor of Mongalla and the Lado Enclave suggested that an 'equatorial battalion' be formed for service in the south; soldiers would be of the Christian faith and the commands given in English. The British administrators immediately saw the value of such a force as a counter-balance to the predominantly Muslim element in the army, and the idea was approved. Over the next few years a unit was raised, although far more animists than Christians were enlisted in its ranks, and it expanded. The Equatoria Corps officially came into being in 1917, its soldiers being all southerners. The last Muslim troops left the south on the 7th December of that year, and from that date onwards, southern soldiers formed the garrisons in the south on a territorial basis.

When Italy entered World War II in June 1940 the Sudan suddenly came into the front line, and the SDF was given the task of patrolling the 2,500-mile long frontier on its east and south, there being only some 2,500 British troops in the country. Opposing them, the Italians had about 300,000 well-equipped troops in Ethiopia and Eritrea, which made some advances across the Sudanese border. The SDF used hit-and-run tactics and carried out extensive patrolling until later in the year British, Commonwealth and Colonial troops arrived to drive the Italians back. By June 1941 the SDF had returned to its normal security duties. It had been a success story in miniature, and the SDF came out of this phase of World War II with high morale. Later, some SDF units served with the British 8th Army in North Africa.

After World War II the process of Sudanization in the SDF was speeded up, more candidates being accepted at the Sudan Military

College, until about sixty officers were graduating annually, but again the large majority were northerners. The SDF also received a few armoured vehicles and some guns. After the Sudan became a republic in 1952, the Egyptian Government's effort to persuade the Sudanese to associate themselves with Egypt caused a split in the officer corps, one faction being in favour of merging with Egypt and the other wanting complete independence.

During the election campaign of 1953 northern politicians made many glib promises which, when they came to power, they could not or did not fulfil. This failure, together with the increasing pace of Sudanization (which to the southerner meant northernization) caused unrest and discontent in the south, and also apprehension as to the Government's intentions. To the southerners it appeared as if they were being colonized for the second time. Both the army and the police in the south—although southerners to a man—were now heavily officered by northerners; of its 33 officers in the Equatoria Corps, the 24 seniors were northerners, leaving only 9 juniors who were southerners. The proportion was much the same in the police and the administration generally.

At the beginning of July 1955 a false telegram, purporting to be signed by Ismail el-Azhari, was circulated in the south, urging the northern administrators to oppress and ill-treat the southerners. It was given much publicity and caused deep anxiety. Doubts now began to be felt about the loyalty of the soldiers in the Equatoria Corps in case of disturbances, and especially if they were ordered to fire upon their own countrymen. The senior northern administrators asked for northern soldiers to be stationed in the south, but this request was turned down by the Government at Khartoum. The senior northern army officers also felt it unnecessary; in their pride and confidence they thought they had firm control over their southern soldiers and commanded their full loyalty.

On the 25th July 1955, after a very dubious trial, a southern member of the National Assembly was imprisoned. This led to demonstrations on the following day in the town of Nazra, in Equatoria province, where 300 southern workers on the Azande Development Scheme had just been dismissed, while extra northern staff had been taken on. Soldiers and police fired upon the demonstrators, killing eight and wounding several. Throughout the July 1955 disturbances in the south the southern policemen had been loyal to their senior northern officers and had carried out their orders, with only one exception at Malakal, in Upper Nile province, but there were now serious doubts about the reliability of the southern soldiers, although no move was made against them for fear of provoking premature action. On the 7th August two southern clerks working with the SDF were arrested and a conspiracy to mutiny was exposed, but the arrests caused an angry mob to form at Juba, which had to be dispersed with tear gas.

These demonstrations caused the alarmed northern administrators to press the Government at Khartoum once again to send northern troops to the south, this time successfully. On the 10th August a detachment of 500 northern soldiers arrived by air at Juba, which then had the only airstrip in the south. The move gave rise to considerable apprehension. It was the Government's intention to station a few detachments of northern troops at strategic points in the south, and to move some, but by no means all, southern soldiers into the north. To put this policy into effect a company at Torit, the HQ of the Equatoria Corps, was ordered to make ready to move northwards, but it became obvious that the soldiers were not willing to obey this order. It was also rumoured that they were to be disarmed. By this time the northern administrators wanted the Equatoria Corps to be disbanded, but this was resisted by the HQ of the SDF in Khartoum, which decided that for the sake of principle and prestige at least one southern company must be moved to Khartoum, and that the order must be enforced.

As was feared, on the 18th, when ordered to mount the trucks that were to take them northwards, the southern soldiers at Torit refused to comply, and instead attacked their officers and broke into the armoury. The mutiny suddenly exploded into violence as the soldiers began killing, burning and looting. Northerners and northern property suffered in particular. On the same day another 190 southern soldiers mutinied in the districts of Juba, Yei, Yambio and Maridi, of whom 138 attempted to link up with the original mutineers by crossing into Uganda with the intention of recrossing into the Sudan nearer Torit, but they were apprehended by the Uganda authorities and disarmed. The other 52 remained at large in western Equatoria. Communications with the north were cut, and on the 19th the Government at Khartoum gave out news of the mutiny, a state of emergency was declared, and more northern soldiers were sent to the south. On the 21st RAF transport aircraft flew to Khartoum, and in all air-lifted about 8,000 soldiers southwards.

41

Mutiny of the Equatoria Corps: 1955

It seems fairly certain that the mutineers, led by Lieutenant Reynaldo Loyela, expected support and encouragement from the British, and they sent telegrams to the British Prime Minister and the GOC British Troops in the Sudan. On the 22nd Premier Azhari called on the mutineers to surrender, but they refused, in turn demanding that northern soldiers be removed from the south. Southern political leaders belatedly came into the picture, unsuccessfully asking for British and Egyptian assistance or intervention. The British Governor-General, Sir Knox Helm, hurried back to the Sudan from leave to send, on the 26th, a warning to the mutineers to surrender, saying he would guarantee them a fair trial. This caused resistance to cease, and the mutiny collapsed the next day.

At a meeting of representatives of both the Government and the mutineers near Juba, it was agreed that the mutineers, who were now all hiding in the forests, would surrender themselves and their arms on the 30th August at Torit, but when northern troops entered Torit on that date they found it to be deserted. Convinced that they would all be killed, or at the best imprisoned, the southern mutineers, fearful and resentful, had disappeared into hiding with their weapons. Their fears were enhanced when it was known that British troops were about to be withdrawn from the Sudan (and indeed all had left by the end of the month), and that they would thus be left entirely at the mercy of the northern soldiers. The suggestion by the Egyptian, Major Saleh Salem, that British troops remain in the Sudan and Egyptian troops be sent there additionally, to maintain order, was rejected by the Azhari Government.

On the 6th September it was stated that order had been restored and that northern troops had occupied Equatoria province, the main seat of the mutiny. The Equatoria Corps was disbanded, but many southern soldiers deserted with their arms, thus forestalling the process, and Muslim troops were stationed in the south on a rotation basis. The northerners blamed the British for the mutiny and disturbances, because they had separated the south from the north for so long, but the immediate causes were the farcical trial of the southern member of the National Assembly and the false telegram that was so widely circulated. Later a commission of enquiry reported the deaths of 261 northerners, the majority (259) in Equatoria province; of these, 55 were drowned in a panic crossing of the Kinyeti River on the 18th, in the general southern exodus from Torit.

Sir Knox Helm left the Sudan on the 15th December 1955, his

post abolished, and so he was unable to implement his promise of fair trials, clemency and safe-conduct. Lieutenant Reynaldo Loyela, the leader of the mutineers, was executed early in 1956. According to one account,[1] thought to be exaggerated, 300 were executed. The only two secondary schools, at Juba and Rumbek, were moved into the north. In 1956 the ban on enlistment of southern soldiers was lifted, but they were expected to serve in the north under northern officers, and few were attracted to such conditions in the climate of fear and distrust that had arisen. The Sudan Police had been centralized in 1953, because the Sudanese police commandants objected to being subordinate to newly promoted Sudanese governors. This lack of local control was blamed by some for the rapid break-down of order in the south and the successes of the mutineers in the following years, when they were able to remain at large and survive.

---

[1] According to *Problems of the Southern Sudan*, by J. Oduhu and W. Deng.

3 *The Republic: 1956–1958*

'In a backward country, prison is the politician's university,
and I have graduated.'

Premier (later President) Ismail al-Azhari

On the 19th December 1955 the Sudanese National Assembly voted
for independence. On the 1st January 1956 the Republic of the
Sudan came into being, and the office of Governor-General ceased,
to be replaced by a five-man Supreme Commission (which included
one southerner, Siricio Iro) as the sovereign power. Later, on the
19th December 1956, the Sudan was admitted to the UN. A period
of almost three years of democratic rule followed, which saw the
formation and development of political parties, coalitions and quarrels. There was already strong rivalry between the two main parties,
the NUP, supported by the Khatmia sect, strong in the cities and
main towns of the north, led by Ismail al-Azhari, and the Umma
Party, supported by the Ansar sect, strong in the countryside and led
by Abdullah Khalil.

In the National Assembly Azhari formed a coalition government,
and became the Sudan's first Premier; he also took on the portfolio
of the Minister of Defence. The NUP suffered from an internal personality conflict, and Azhari maintained his leadership by ruthlessly
eliminating men who disagreed with him or who questioned his
decisions. He also alienated members of his supporting Khatmia sect.
The only two southern members of his Government were Bullen
Alier and Buth Diu, who were soon dismissed for disagreeing with
his southern policy.

In June 1956 the People's Democratic Party (PDP) was formed
in the National Assembly by Khatmia members, who broke away
from the NUP owing to disagreements with Azhari and also because
a split had occurred between those who favoured complete Sudanese
independence, and those who wanted closer links with Egypt. Twenty-
one National Assembly Members of the NUP changed their allegiance to the PDP, which was led by Murghani Hamza.

Both the Umma Party and the new PDP voted against Azhari,

who lost his former coalition majority. On the 5th July 1956 Abdullah Khalil, leader of the Umma Party, became Premier, forming a temporary coalition with the PDP. Khalil's Umma Party stood for 'positive neutrality', and he fended off attempts by the Egyptians, Russians and Americans to gain influence in the Sudan. The Russians then thought of the Sudan as the 'gateway to Africa'. In 1957 Premier Khalil refused the Soviet offer to take the unsold portion of the Sudanese cotton crop in exchange for Soviet arms, saying he wanted agricultural machinery and not tanks; neither would he allow the Soviet Union to stage an 'Atoms for Peace' exhibition in Khartoum. In April 1957 he rejected proffered aid under the Eisenhower doctrine, but later that year he did accept some American technical assistance. The suspicious Premier Khalil checked on every army officer, government official and many others, to ascertain their political views and connexions, if any.

Southern members of the National Assembly, on the 19th December 1955, had voted with Azhari for independence, because they had been promised that 'full consideration' would be given to their claim for federal status for the south—an expression which was to cause later argument. The southerners soon became disillusioned and disappointed with the Azhari Government, but they should not have expected much, as at the beginning of 1955, with an NUP delegation, Azhari had toured the south in attempts to dampen down the desire for federal status and to counter the growing popularity of the Southern Party's political platform. His views on the matter were never disguised, and he later stated[1] that 'The Sudan should be one unit on the basis of the decision arrived at during the Juba Conference of 1947.' During 1955 southern members of the National Assembly were demanding that a plebiscite be held under the auspices of the United Nations, but neither Azhari nor the British would allow this. There was also discontent about the economic neglect of the south. The post-World War II cotton boom had brought large profits to the Sudan and much of the money was spent on agricultural, irrigation and other development projects, but the majority of them were in the north, while the main one in the south, the Azande Development Scheme, had already been cut back.

Continued southern disappointment, complaints and demands for federal status led Premier Azhari on the 19th December 1956, as a

[1] According to the Report of the Commission of Enquiry into the Disturbances in Southern Sudan during August 1955 (Khartoum, 1956).

sop, to pass a resolution in the National Assembly which promised a form of federation to the south and to set up a constitutional committee to examine and report upon the possibility of a federal structure, but of its 46 members only three were southerners, who were always hopelessly outvoted. When Khalil became Premier he repudiated this December 1956 resolution, and his Umma Party–PDP coalition continued to use repressive measures in the south and to ignore protests and warnings. To maintain his position Premier Khalil relied upon the support of the PDP, which was firmly against a federal solution. In December 1957 it was announced that the constitutional committee 'had given the southern claim for federation very serious consideration, and found that it would not work in this country'. The three dissenting southern members had long since withdrawn from the committee.

In 1957 Izbone Mendiri, a southern member of the National Assembly, formed the Southern Federal Party, which was to vote in opposition with the NUP. This new party's objectives were the recognition of English and Christianity equally with Arabic and Islam, the establishment of an independent southern army, and a separate southern programme of economic development. The National Assembly was dissolved on the 30th June 1957 to prepare for elections, which were held from the 27th February to the 9th March 1958. The main issue in the north was what degree of co-operation, if any, should be given to Egypt. The southern problem scarcely attracted their attention, although both Saturnino Lohure and Elia Lupe of the Federal Party openly campaigned for complete autonomy for the south. The result of the election was that the Umma Party gained 63 seats, the NUP 45, the PDP 27, the Southern Bloc 37, and the Anti-Imperialist Front 1.[1] The wing of the Southern Party, led by Stanislaus Paysama, had been so successful that he was again able to form all southern members of the National Assembly into a Southern Bloc for voting purposes. The President of the Southern Bloc was initially Saturnino Lohure, a priest, and the Secretary-General was Luigi Adwok. Three southern ministers were appointed to the new Khalil Government, Lohure, Adwok and Mendiri. Izbone Mendiri was sentenced to imprisonment for incitement, and both Lohase and Adwok resigned, to be replaced by Elijah Mayen and Franco Garang.

[1] Some authorities quote the 'Southern Bloc' as gaining 40 out of 46 southern seats, but this figure includes members of northern parties, and tends to confuse.

Once the constitutional committee had rejected the possibility of federation outright (in December 1957) the Southern Bloc began to make serious contact with the African (as opposed to the Arab peoples) in the north—of which there were about three million—to encourage them to demand the right to manage their own affairs. A good response came from the Beja, the Fur, the Nuba and the Funj. The idea of federation spread and began to find favour amongst certain majority groups in the north. For example, the Beja Congress in August 1958 insisted that Premier Khalil visit them to discuss this demand, while similar proposals were put forward by other groups, such as the Social Organization of the Nuba Mountains, which had been formed in 1954. Azhari, in his quest for popularity and power, gave some vague degree of support to the idea of federation.

Troubles were crowding in on Premier Khalil thick and fast. The cotton crop of 1958 was a poor one, and difficulty in disposing of it caused the Sudan's foreign exchange reserves to fall dangerously low. This and other matters precipitated a political crisis. During October the Government was attacked by Azhari, leader of the opposition NUP, which favoured closer links with Egypt, for its failure to cope with the crisis, and in particular for accepting British military aid;[1] Azhari alleged that this aligned the Sudan too closely with the West. On the 27th political meetings and demonstrations were banned in Khartoum and Omdurman because of disturbances after Azhari had openly compared Premier Khalil with the recently assassinated, pro-Western Premier of Iraq, Nuri es-Said. Murghani Hamza, leader of the PDP, also openly criticized Khalil for accepting British aid. The PDP was splitting away from the coalition because a section of the Umma Party wanted to make the Sudan an Islamic kingdom, with the Mahdi, Abdul Rahman, as the first king, a course the PDP strongly opposed.

Premier Khalil was also involved in a dispute with President Nasser of Egypt over the distribution of the Nile waters; in July Khalil had held back far more than the agreed share.[2] Now that he had obtained Soviet aid to carry on with his Aswan Dam project, Nasser was anxious to make a firm agreement on this matter, and

---

[1] On the 18th October 1958 the British Foreign Office announced that a quantity of arms and equipment (unspecified) was being sent to the Sudan, and also that 'free' training was being given to some Sudanese pilots.

[2] By an agreement of 1929, Egypt was to have twelve-thirteenths of the Nile waters.

early in November both Premier Khalil and Murghani Hamza went to Cairo for talks with the Egyptian President.

By his thoughtless treatment of the southern problem, Premier Khalil had lost the support of the southern members of the National Assembly, which he desperately needed at this moment. To avoid a vote of 'no confidence', which would bring down his Government, he adjourned the National Assembly until the 17th November. In the past southern members had on occasions boycotted the National Assembly, mainly in protest at their gross under-representation on the constitutional committee. On the 14th November Khalil held consultations with other parties in an attempt to form an all-party government, but these failed, so he again adjourned the meeting of the National Assembly until the 8th December. In addition to all these difficulties faced by the Sudanese Premier, in November there were signs in the south that the 'mutineers', who had been hiding in the forests since 1955, were about to emerge and commence guerilla warfare against the northern administration. The situation was such that it was barely surprising that Premier Khalil, almost unprotestingly, allowed power to be snatched from his grasp by the army, led by Brigadier Abboud.

The brief period of sickly democratic rule ended abruptly just before it might have smashed itself to pieces. Beset as the governments were by internal conflicts, their record was marred by fractionalism, nepotism, corruption and the behaviour of self-seeking politicians. The British had set up and handed over to the Sudanese a form of government based on the Westminster model, but since 1956 no government had been strong enough to govern properly. The main reasons for the failure had been partly because the personality cult obtruded so much, and partly because some of the prominent leaders, such as Azhari and Khalil—there were others too —wanted to replace the British-type parliamentary government with a presidential one with the President—as in America—having full executive authority. Visualizing themselves as future presidents, several strove unsuccessfully towards that goal, and in the process democracy crumbled and the country suffered. In the south there was northern repression, a military occupation by Muslim soldiers, government by an Arabic-speaking administration, and an apprehensive, sullen population.

In the early hours of the 17th November 1958 armoured vehicles surrounded Khartoum, soldiers occupied the airport, radio station and all government buildings, and sentries were posted outside foreign embassies. It was a bloodless coup as the army, led by Brigadier Abboud, Commander-in-Chief of the Sudanese armed forces, had moved in to seize power from the quarrelling politicians. There were no disturbances or disruption of normal life. Premier Khalil and members of his Government were awakened early and given letters dismissing them from their posts. A dawn announcement over the radio told the people that the army had assumed power to end corruption and chaos. A state of emergency was declared, the constitution was suspended, and the National Assembly and all political parties were dissolved. The Supreme Council, which had head of state powers, was dismissed and its place was taken by the Supreme Council of the Armed Forces, headed by Brigadier Abboud.

On the next day, the 18th, Brigadier Abboud said at a press conference that the time was not yet ripe for Western democracy for the Sudan, that the armed forces did not want to hold power for ever, and that he hoped it would be possible for a form of democracy to be restored within six to twelve months. He is reported to have said later: 'I am not a politician. I have been busy with military matters, and haven't studied these things.' The press was allowed to remain uncensored on the condition it did not print anything subversive about the new regime. The coup had happened so smoothly, so suddenly and so efficiently, that there was considerable speculation whether there had been collusion between Premier Khalil and Brigadier Abboud, who were personal friends. Khalil was also related to Brigadier Wahab, who became Abboud's deputy. Only twelve members of the Anti-Imperialist Front and five members of the Trade Union Federation, both organizations being regarded as Communist motivated, were arrested. Apart from this, there were no other arrests and no trials of politicians. Both Abdul Rahman al-Mahdi, leader of the Ansar sect, and Ali al-Murghani, leader of the Khatmia sect, expressed their approval of the coup.

On the same day, the 18th, a new Government was formed, headed by Brigadier Abboud, consisting of seven officers and five civilians, all non-party men. The only southerner was Santino Deng, who was Minister of Animal Resources, a job he had held under Premier Khalil. Abboud said that he had taken over the country to 'combat deteriorating democracy'. Certainly the Sudan had swung from one extreme to the other—from democracy to military dictatorship, that hardened quickly, the excuse being that a strong government was needed to negotiate with Egypt. The new regime was quickly recognized by foreign powers, and on the 30th November it in turn recognized China. It also negotiated an $18-million barter agreement with the Communist bloc, and became friendly with the West, obtaining aid, loans and credits from Britain, West Germany and America.

Ibrahim Abboud, who became the Premier and Defence Minister, was born in 1900, in the Red Sea coastal region, of the Hadendowa tribe (the original fuzzy-wuzzies of Kipling). He was a career soldier who, after attending the Gordon College, entered the SDF in 1924. During World War II he served in Eritrea and Libya, after which he commanded the Camel Corps, being appointed Deputy Commander-in-Chief in 1954 and Commander-in-Chief in 1956. His deputy in the Government in all respects was Brigadier Ahmed Abdul Wahab. Wahab had entered the SDF in 1938, and had served in Eritrea during World War II, being appointed Deputy Commander-in-Chief just a few months before the coup. Neither man had been concerned in politics before.

4 *The Rise of Southern Nationalism*

'The Sudanese nation is still at the rear of the
caravan of progress.'
Time of the 6th July 1959

Meanwhile, discontent with the Muslim administration and army of occupation in the south was deepening, and there were increasing incidents involving the 'mutineers' lurking in the forests and the Government troops who were seeking them out. As yet the 'rebels', or 'outlaws' as the Khartoum Government officially designated them, were few in number and they lacked cohesion, organization and central direction; their scarce firearms were the old British rifles and sten-guns they had taken with them when they had deserted. The people in the south could not be said to identify themselves even vaguely with the 'rebels', and in 1957, in the Yei district, it was something of a surprise when the army blew up some 700 huts as a punishment for sheltering 'rebels'. Some looked upon this as the first sign of the population attempting to form the 'sea' which the 'fish', the guerilla fighter, needs in which to 'swim', but it is far more likely that the people had been forced to harbour the 'rebels' at gun-point. At this stage the population was as frightened of the 'rebels', who stole their food and thoughtlessly ill-treated them, as of the Government troops.

The missionaries were suspected by the Government of helping, and even inciting the 'rebels', and of actively opposing the Government's integration policy. No doubt some of them became involved to a degree, feeling that they were simply doing what they could to keep back the seeping tide of Islam and to protect their flocks. Sadik al-Mahdi, who became the leader of the Umma Party,[1] rejecting the use of force in the south, had advocated that the spread of Islam would solve the problem, so the missionaries had need to be wary. There were just over a quarter of a million black Christians in the south, although the missionaries liked to insist that they

[1] The Mahdi, Abdul Rahman, died on the 24th March 1959, and was succeeded by his son, Sadik.

numbered over half a million. A fairly reliable estimate was thought to be 270,251,[1] while another reliable one was that of about 200,000 Roman Catholics and 30,000 Protestants.

Unconsciously influenced by traditional military prejudice against 'mutineers', at first President Abboud refused to believe that a basic southern problem existed. Convinced that the missionaries were simply trouble-making, he clamped further restrictions on them and their work. He was encouraged in this belief because the southern refugees, especially those in Uganda, were supported by the Sudanese Christian Association, which was backed by several foreign church organizations. In 1957 the schools in the south had been nationalized, and all privately owned ones, that is missionary schools, were prohibited. In 1960 the Sunday weekly holiday was abolished, and all had to revert to the Muslim Friday. On the 15th May 1962 the Missionary Societies Act required missionaries to obtain licences from the Government within six months, and they were forbidden to proselytize, except under restrictions.

In 1961 a spate of incidents occurred in the south, some of which involved the 'rebels', but others—the majority—concerned old-style tribal dissidence and rivalry; for example, there was unrest amongst the Anuak, along the Baro Salient, many of whom fled into Ethiopia. President Abboud felt that force would solve the matter, and he met all signs of disorder or dissidence in the south with stern, and often savage, reprisals. Rumours of a guerilla-type force being formed in the forests, together with the general disturbances in 1961 and 1962, and the consequent reprisals, caused the pupils in southern schools, now Government-controlled, to stay away, in case they might become targets for Government action. The schools never functioned properly again before they were all finally closed in 1964.

A few southern senior officials still remained at their posts in the south. The most prominent was William Deng, an Assistant District Commissioner at Kapoeta, who was regarded as being loyal to Government policy, especially as in January 1960 he had written an article for a magazine supporting the idea of complete integration of the south. However, he soon became disillusioned, or something went wrong, as later that year he defected and left the country. He alleged that he was obstructed in his work and given no help, that all records had been removed when he had temporarily taken over

[1] According to *The Middle East and North Africa 1964–5* (Europa Publications, London).

the Torit District, and that he was the victim of nepotism, as an overseas course of instruction he was expecting to be sent on had been suddenly given to someone else. The Government spokesman stated that Deng had defected in a fit of pique, and so no special significance should be attached to his action, but nevertheless, all remaining southern officials were immediately transferred to the north.

The abolition of political parties in the Sudan was a blow to southern aspirations, as this order muted southern politicians, and indeed some southern ex-members of the National Assembly. Several prominent southerners were called into the Government office at Juba and warned to stop talking about independence or federation. All dialogue with the north ceased. In 1959 Dominic Muerwel, a former southern member of the National Assembly, was arrested when about to leave the country with the intention of setting up a southern political movement in exile. He was sentenced to ten years' imprisonment (but quietly released in 1962). It was alleged that he was beaten-up and ill-treated to such an extent that he had to spend eight months in hospital.

The majority of southern political leaders remained in the open in the south, although there were frequent arrests, until in early December 1960 it was discovered that the Government was mounting an operation to seize and detain them all on Christmas Day, the intention being to 'behead' the political movement that wanted independence or federation. Scenting danger, the southern leaders went underground and quietly slipped away into exile, thus starting what escalated into large-scale migrations of southern refugees into adjacent Uganda, Kenya, Ethiopia and the Central African Republic, which grew in volume as fear was generated by Abboud's reprisal policy.

In February 1962 prominent southern leaders in exile formed the Sudan African Closed Districts National Union (SACDNU) at Kinshasa (then Leopoldville) in Zaire (then the Belgian Congo). Joseph Oduhu became its first President, Marko Rume its Vice-President and William Deng its Secretary-General, with Aggrey Jaden as its Assistant Secretary-General. Active in its affairs, and perhaps the real leader, was Saturnino Lohure, who assumed the title of 'Patron'. In 1963, after his release from a Sudanese prison, Dominic Muerwal replaced Marko Rume as the Vice-President. The policy of SACDNU was to obtain complete independence for the south, and this was to be achieved by diplomatic and political means. Joseph Oduhu, the

President, openly disclaimed the use of force, or any connexion with the 'armed rebels' lurking in the southern forests. The SACDNU provided information for the press and sent petitions to the UN and the Organization of African Unity (OAU), urging them to support the south in its struggle against the north. It would have liked both the UN and the OAU to intervene in the south, but neither organization responded.

In 1963 the SACDNU changed its name to the Sudan African National Union (SANU), which after initial temporary moves set up its HQ in Kampala, Uganda, where there were already numbers of southern refugees—no one knew exactly how many at this stage. However, the SANU leadership was not united, there were divergent views, personalities clashed, and personal ambitions protruded. For example, an element of SANU, influenced by William Deng, had remained behind at Kinshasa for a while.

Meanwhile, in the north, although he adopted a pose of benevolent dictator, incorruptible father-figure, forced against his will to rule his country for its own good (an image that was originally easily projected because of his mildness and clemency in his bloodless coup), President Abboud soon began to have his full share of trouble, some from his own officers, who were either dissatisfied with his policy or who wanted to topple him to take his place. At least two brigadiers had been left out of Abboud's Government and they were aggrieved; on the 2nd March 1959 one of them, Brigadier Abdul Rahman Shenan, in charge of the Northern Command,[1] sent two of his companies of soldiers into Khartoum to present President Abboud with his demands for recognition and reward, after which his soldiers withdrew from the city. As these demands did not appear to have been met, before dawn on the 4th a unit of Brigadier Shenan's again entered Khartoum, surrounded the Presidential Palace, cordoned off the Defence Ministry building, occupied key points and arrested Brigadier Wahab and two other members of the Supreme Council. Brigadier Shenan was joined by some troops from the Eastern Command, the officer in charge being another aggrieved brigadier, Moheiddin Ahmed Abdullah, and a few from the Khartoum garrison itself. President Abboud bowed before the pressure, and in the evening announced in a radio broadcast that he accepted the resignation of the Supreme Council of the Armed Forces, and

[1] The Sudanese army had been reorganized into territorial commands after independence.

had called a conference with senior military officers for the following day. Abboud had no option but to include three brigadiers who had been privy to his coup.

On the next day, the 5th, a new Supreme Council of ten members, headed by Abboud, was formed. It included Brigadier Shenan, Brigadier Moheiddin Ahmed Abdullah and the other brigadier who was in charge of the West Central Command, Makboul al-Amin, who were pro-Egyptian and were regarded as Arab nationalists. Wahab was included too. However, at the first meeting of the new Supreme Council on the 9th, Brigadier Wahab, who was considered to be pro-Western, was dismissed, and the three brigadiers, Shenan, Abdullah and Amin, became ministers in Abboud's Government. The changes were officially put down to 'differences between senior army officers over purely internal matters'. It was in fact simply a matter of the division of the spoil.

All seemed to go well with the Government for a couple of months, and then there was more military trouble for Abboud. On the night of the 21st May 1959 a unit of soldiers from the Eastern Command began moving with four armoured vehicles on Khartoum. The coup misfired right from the start, when the officer in charge of transport refused to join in and allow his vehicles to be used to lift the troops. Sensing failure, Brigadier Abdullah, one of the senior plotters, rushed out in an attempt to stop the soldiers who had begun marching on foot, but he failed to make contact with them. However, another senior plotter was able to do this, and the troops turned about and returned to their HQ, being told that 'their grievances' would be looked into. By this time President Abboud had been alerted as to what was going on and he immediately ordered the arrest of Brigadiers Shenan and Abdullah. Other arrests followed. This time the coup had failed because the Supreme Council as a body had stood firm, and soldiers from other commands and the Khartoum garrison had refused to join in, although some junior officers were said to have been eager to have done so had they been able. On the 26th May twenty-four leading members of the illegal Communist Party were detained. In the mid-1940s some Sudanese students had formed a study group within the Egyptian Communist Party, which later developed into the independent Sudanese Communist Party and for a while called itself the Sudanese Movement of National Liberation.

Two series of courts martial followed. The first began on the 21st

June when Brigadiers Shenan and Abdullah were charged with inciting and conspiring to launch an armed attack on Khartoum, and of attempting to overthrow the regime. On the 24th June Major-General Abdullah Hamid, who had given evidence, was arrested, to be tried with the second batch. That trial opened on the 22nd July. In all, some twenty-nine officers of the Northern and Eastern Commands were arraigned, and the nation listened to the entire proceedings over the radio. On the 22nd September the verdicts were announced. Brigadiers Shenan and Abdullah and four other senior officers were found guilty and sentenced to death, but these punishments were commuted to life imprisonment by President Abboud, while General Hamid, who was accused of being nominated to head a new Supreme Council, was simply dismissed from the army. The remaining officers found guilty were dismissed from the army also, and additionally some were imprisoned. President Abboud had survived this power tussle within the armed forces, and retained his benevolent dictator image. Even so, clearly all was not well within the army. On the 9th November 1959 there was a brief, unsuccessful attempt to stage a coup at the School of Infantry, then at Omdurman, led by Lieutenant Ali Hamid. Later Ali Hamid and four others were hanged instead of being shot, as it was feared that the soldiers might refuse to obey the order to fire at the executions. Others were sent to prison.

President Abboud was concerned about his country's relations with Egypt, but he was practical and clear-sighted. On the 8th November 1959 he concluded a new Nile Waters Agreement, by which the Sudan retained two-thirds of the water. On the occasion of the second anniversary of the Abboud regime, President Nasser visited the Sudan (from the 15th to the 25th November 1960). While he was there Abboud announced that he was going to re-organize the system of government as there was too much power concentrated in the hands of the central government, provincial governors and district commissioners, and that elections would be held for new councils. These measures were rather slow in coming into effect. On the 20th December 1962 Abboud, who retained the posts and titles of President of the Supreme Council of the Armed Forces, Premier, Defence Minister and Commander-in-Chief, made an extensive Government reshuffle. In the following year, 1963, on the 26th April, elections were held for local councils, and on the 12th October for the provincial councils. The Central Council was formally inaugurated by President Abboud on the 14th November.

5 *The Anya-Nya Emerges*

'We will never hesitate to go back to our barracks at any moment that we are satisfied that good government is established.'

President Ibrahim Abboud

While southern politicians in exile were quarrelling amongst themselves, inside the south an embryo guerilla army was slowly being knocked into shape by its own military leaders, and without the aid or interference of southern politicians, who since 1960 were divorced from it. Some 500 soldiers of the former Equatoria Corps—both the original '1955 mutineers' and those who deserted through fear—had remained more or less intact in small groups, some of which had developed upon a tribal or regional basis, dependent upon where they found themselves or to where, in the forests they gravitated for safety. Continually pressed by Government troops, they were compelled to retain a semblance of military unity and discipline to survive. In fact, the period from 1955 until 1963 was simply one of guerilla survival, scarcely removed from banditry, and that it was successful was due to a score or so of former southern army officers and warrant officers, and a small number of former non-commissioned officers. It could be said that this was the 'bandit period', as they foraged for food in an aggressive way. At this time there was still more of a sense of injustice and injury than of political awakening. The men were more bandits than a cohesive, politically stimulated guerilla force. They were still hunted 'outlaws' and 'rebels', rather than skilful guerilla fighters with a set purpose and aim.

Except for perhaps just under 200 weapons they had no firearms and little ammunition, and so they had to rely upon primitive tribal bows and arrows, spears and machetes. This 'forest' army was increased in 1961, when some 800 southerners, who had been sentenced to imprisonment after the 1955 mutiny, were released from prison and, having no skills, no jobs and no prospects, mostly drifted to join the 'rebels' in the forests, which meant that its strength was now well over the thousand mark. But it was in widely scattered autono-

57

NEWS REPORTS

From Equatoria, South Sudan

KHARTOUM THREATENS THE SOUTH

LAST WARNING

1. WE KNOW THAT SOME OF YOU ARE HELPING THE OUTLAWS WITH FOOD, SHELTER, MEDICINE AND INFORMATION— WILLINGLY OR UNWILLINGLY.
2. WE KNOW THAT THE OUTLAWS ARE MISGUIDING YOU FOR THEIR OWN PERSONAL INTERESTS.

TO THOSE — THIS IS OUR LAST WARNING

1. COME BACK AND ASSIST IN BUILDING YOUR COUNTRY IN PEACE. DO NOT RISK YOUR LIFE, YOUR FAMILY AND YOUR HOME FOR NOTHING.
2. YOU CAN STILL HAVE A JOB, A FARM AND EDUCATION FOR YOU AND YOUR FAMILY.
3. REPORT TO ANY ARMY, POLICE OR LOCAL AUTHORITY, AND YOU ARE SAFE UNDER THE AMNESTY LAW AND THE REGIONAL AUTONOMY PROGRAMMES.
4. THE ARMED FORCES ARE WELL EQUIPPED AND ABLE TO REACH THE OUTLAWS' CAMPS ANYWHERE, ANY TIME.
5. RAIDS AND ATTACKS WILL CONTINUE ON THESE CAMPS AND THE OUTLAWS WILL HAVE NO PEACE OR REST DAY AND NIGHT.

ANSWER THE CALL AND REPORT NOW

(This is a true copy of leaflets recently dropped in South Sudan)

Example of a leaflet dropped by the Government

mous groups. The men had little knowledge or comprehension of guerilla warfare as such, but their hatred of northerners manifested itself in the occasional ambush, shooting incident or minor attack. After the disturbances of 1961 and 1962, which mainly concerned tribal dissidence and quarrels, there was a comparative lull, occasioned largely by Abboud's harsh reprisal policy.

The military and militant leaders still in the south came to realize that all peaceful means had failed, and that dictatorship debarred dialogue. They realized that to achieve independence they would have to fight for it, and a number of them met together to formulate policy. At this stage the several military leaders, while having some form of liaison with each other, were very much a law unto themselves. This situation mitigated against unity, but in September 1963 a group of them attended a conference at a forest camp where, on the 19th, they decided to merge their forces; the combined organization was to be called the Land Freedom Army (LFA) and their soldiers called Freedom Fighters. The LFA was to be based on the British model, with British-type formations, ranks and words of command—the only ones they knew. A Commander-in-Chief, 'Major-General' Emilio Tafeng, was appointed. He was a former Lieutenant in the SDF, commissioned from the ranks. Other appointments of *de facto* existing territorial commanders were confirmed, and appropriate ranks bestowed. General Tafeng and half a dozen of his senior regional commanders met together periodically.

Soon the LFA adopted the name of 'Anya-Nya', which means in the Madi, Moru and Lotuko languages 'snake poison'.[1] The Madi tribe inhabited the southern sector of Equatoria province adjacent to the Uganda border between Nimule and Juba, an area in which the shifting GHQ hovered. Later an Anya-Nya badge was evolved, depicting a charging buffalo surrounded by two snakes, the whole split by an arrow, signifying the strength of the buffalo, the deadliness of the snake and the accuracy of an arrow. The Anya-Nya began to establish small base and training camps in the less accessible border terrain in countries adjacent to the southern borders, and just within the frontiers. Attention was given to improving command and liaison between GHQ and senior commanders, and also to recruitment and training.

The Anya-Nya talked about rather than deliberately planned a

---

[1] According to Oliver Albino, it means literally the 'venom of the Gabon viper' but Mahgoub refers to it as a 'poisonous insect'.

guerilla warfare campaign against the occupying Muslim army and administration, which was to include blowing bridges, blocking roads, ambushing northern troops and punishing southerners who collaborated with the Government or who would not help the Anya-Nya. Once it got spasmodically under way, it proved to be a hard programme and a ruthless one that caused considerable hardship and suffering to the ordinary people who were caught between two fires, as Government troops would burn down villages and huts as a punishment for harbouring or helping the Anya-Nya, while the LFA razed them for allegedly collaborating with the northerners. This resulted in an enormous increase in the number of refugees, who consisted not only of those with political or militant ideas, but hordes of ordinary people. Ravaged villages were deserted as the inhabitants fled into the forests.

The first serious guerilla attacks occurred in September 1963 but they were not part of this new Anya-Nya campaign, being instigated by William Deng. In the first, on the 9th, a small Anya-Nya force assaulted and overran a police post at Pachola, near the Ethiopian border. The Anya-Nya claimed it as a three-day fight, followed by one week of occupation. The second occurred on the 19th, when another police post at Kajo Kaji, near the Uganda border, was overrun. In both incidents several police were killed.

The next assault, which was launched on the barracks at Wau, the capital of Bahr el-Ghazal province on the 11th January 1964, was led by 'Captain' Bernandino, a missionary-educated Dinka, who commanded 123 'uniformed' Freedom Fighters, armed with British rifles and sten-guns and Molotov cocktails. The attempt was abortive and was beaten off by the northern garrison, which had been alerted by a prematurely sounded Anya-Nya bugle call, before the Freedom Fighters were ready in their positions to start the assault. Captain Bernandino and sixty of his men were captured. On the 23rd February he and two others (a former prison warder and an ex-soldier of the Equatoria Corps) were hanged, while others were sentenced to imprisonment. This opening shot of the Anya-Nya guerilla campaign had badly misfired, and was a setback that took some time to overcome, causing morale to be shaken and making the Freedom Fighters timid about attacking northern positions, no matter how small.

A letter from William Deng was found on Bernandino when captured, appointing him a 'captain' in the Land Freedom Army, and authorizing him to plan the assault on Wau. With the dissolution of the National Assembly, the SANU claimed the right to an internationally supervised plebiscite. To bring this demand to international notice, William Deng had organized a series of armed raids into the south from adjacent countries, hoping that hasty reaction by Abboud's troops would cause 'incidents' that would somehow attract UN involvement. Small groups of the original 'mutineers' were used for this purpose, and they raided into the south, attacking isolated police and frontier posts with the object of acquiring arms for themselves. At the time the continued presence of the UN Force in adjacent Congo was in doubt, so it was necessary for Deng, if he was to 'internationalize' the southern issue in this manner, to cause some major 'border incident' to happen while there was still a UN force in Central Africa potentially able to intervene.

After his failure to embroil the UN force or to attract world attention in this way, William Deng, once he had virtually launched what developed into the Anya-Nya rebellion, made little effort to control or direct it.[1] Perhaps it was an almost impossible task at this stage, owing to the huge distances involved and a lack of communications. But possibly the main reason was his total immersion in politics and a consequent lack of time or inclination for the purely military side of the struggle.

Southern politicians in exile were forever angling to gain authority over the Anya-Nya, but as all political activity was banned in the south, the SANU was not represented on the ground and so the field was left clear for the Anya-Nya leaders to conduct operations as, when, and how they pleased. Also, officially at this stage, the SANU was dedicated to peaceful means to obtain its objectives, and it was not until September 1964 when the potential of the Land Freedom Army became obvious, that the SANU changed its policy, ceased to condemn violence, and instead openly sought to gain control of the southern guerilla army in the field, such as it was.

Despite the failure at Wau, the Anya-Nya launched a series of small guerilla incidents, not all of which were plain banditry, over a wide sector during the remainder of the year, although the emphasis seems to have been on recruiting, training and regularizing formations. By the end of 1964 the Anya-Nya was slightly more than a mere semblance of a guerilla force, which is far more than it had

[1] According to Keith Kyle, in *The Southern Problem in the Sudan; The World Today* of December 1966.

been so far. Its strength may have been over 2,000. Recruiting had been restricted because of shortage of weapons, but morale had tended to rise.

The Anya-Nya attack on Wau caused the Government to rush more troops to the south and clamp more restrictions on movement. On the 12th February 1964 many southern police, prison staff and minor officials were arrested, and later 105 of them were tried and sentenced to imprisonment on subversive charges, while practically all the remaining southerners in Government employment were ordered to move to the north. The sudden surge of southern nationalism was such that the majority of them deserted and joined the Anya-Nya, leaving an almost wholly Muslim army and administration, which gave an even more outward appearance of 'foreign occupation'. The strength of the Sudanese army had been increased to over 20,000, and consisted basically of four infantry brigades, one of which had been stationed in Equatoria province since 1955, being periodically reinforced as required. More units were sent into the other two southern provinces, especially that of Bahr el-Ghazal, until it was estimated there were well over 8,000 northern soldiers in the south.

President Abboud reacted to the Anya-Nya attack on Wau by expelling on the 27th February 300 foreign missionaries (272 Roman Catholics and 28 Protestants) because, he alleged, they were misleading and inciting southerners and causing trouble. Missions and churches were free to carry on provided they were taken over by Sudanese clergy. Previously, in 1962, nearly 100 foreign missionaries had been expelled, and another 143 in 1963; the reason then given was that they had become redundant as teachers and were being replaced by Sudanese. It was also announced, in February 1964, that foreign merchants would be allowed to reside only in provincial or district capitals, where they could be under surveillance, and not in the villages, a restriction aimed mainly at Syrian and Greek traders, who were suspected of helping the 'rebels'.

The Sudanese Government alleged that the Wau attack had been planned and mounted from a guerilla camp just over the border in Zaire, and that its Government was aware of what was happening, and was knowingly harbouring the Sudanese 'rebels'. There was some truth in these allegations but, as yet, none in the rumours that the Israelis (who maintained a military and training mission in Uganda and who were probing the 'soft under-belly' of the hostile

Muslim bloc in north-east Africa) were helping to train the Anya-Nya. On the 8th May 1964 Sudanese soldiers crossed over into the Republic of Zaire to attack an Anya-Nya camp, near the town of Aba, from where it was thought the Wau assault had been launched. The position in Uganda was also obscure, as while its Government gave refuge to many southerners, it gave no military aid at all to the Land Freedom Army; indeed, in Kampala in February 1964, Joseph Oduhu, President of the SANU, was detained for trying to recruit southerners from the refugee camps for the Anya-Nya. In that month William Deng, the Secretary-General of the SANU, hastily left Uganda and returned to Kinshasa, from where the Sudanese Government attempted to extradite him. Deng then went to Geneva to carry out a propaganda campaign against the Abboud regime. During his absence in Europe Joseph Oduhu gained authority within the SANU. William Deng was inclined to make arbitrary decisions in the name of the SANU without proper consultations, which upset many of his colleagues, with whom he was invariably in disagreement over his individualistic activities.

Large numbers of southern refugees had also fled over the border into Ethiopia, but on the 3rd May 1964 President Abboud concluded an extradition treaty with Emperor Haile Selassie, at a moment when relations between those two countries were better than customary. The treaty did not mean very much; nothing happened in fact and no one was extradited. The SANU made protests to the UN, alleging that people in the six southern districts of the south were being exterminated by Government troops, who occasionally followed refugees over the Ethiopian border. The SANU also alleged that fourteen southern refugee settlements in Ethiopia had been burned down by Sudanese soldiers, and that Ethiopia was about to return 4,000 refugees to the Sudan. This treaty caused an exodus from Ethiopia into both Kenya and Uganda. There were several instances of Government troops pursuing the Freedom Fighters, and those suspected of helping them, over national borders.

On the 6th May 1964[1] there were reported to be 60,000 southern refugees in Uganda, of whom 7,000 had arrived in the last few days, together with 16,000 cattle and 15,000 sheep. Another report[2] stated that the Uganda-Sudan frontier had been closed, and that there were 50,000 southern refugees in Uganda and 25,000 still in Ethiopia,

---

[1] According to the *Glasgow Herald* of the 6th May 1964.
[2] According to the *Daily Telegraph* of the 7th May 1964.

while yet another report gave a figure of only 11,000 southern refugees in Uganda. Estimates of numbers of refugees varied so widely that it is not possible even to try to assess them accurately; it can simply be said that they amounted to 'several thousands'. Tardily the UN, in May 1964, made an initial grant of £175,000 to the Sudanese refugees in Uganda.

Sufficient guerilla incidents occurred to cause northern troops to take severe reprisals, and reports of other excesses also came in, especially concerning the area surrounding Torit. It also became clear that although the Anya-Nya still clung to its tendency to plain banditry, it was making an effort to curb this private adventurism, and where successful, the people had begun to look more favourably on the Freedom Fighters. It could not be said that the revolt was taking on the character of a popular one, fully supported by all the people, but the seed was being sown. Because of Anya-Nya activities during 1964, which made travel unsafe and life and property insecure, practically all the northerners living and working in the south—with the exception of Government employees of one sort or another—left and returned to the north. Government officials usually spent a two-year tour of duty in the south, and were extremely glad to return home when it had been completed.

Northern public opinion became restless at the growing chaotic situation in the south, and the failure of President Abboud to solve the problem, which now seemed to have escalated from simple banditry and lawlessness to guerilla warfare with all its implications, but the northern politicians were far more interested in ending the military regime than in solving the southern problem. However, indirectly and unexpectedly, the southern problem caused the fall of the Abboud Government. When, on the 7th September 1964, a commission of enquiry was set up to report on the 'unrest' in the south, it appealed to citizens to submit their views on the problem. This chink in the heavy curtain of censorship caused the students of Khartoum University, instigated by the Left, to organize themselves into groups for discussion. In addition to talking about the southern problem they criticized all aspects of the Abboud Government and defied orders not to express opinions except before the commission. The commission, which consisted of thirteen northern and thirteen southern members, was to make recommendations with the object of 'consolidating confidence and achieving stability', but it was not to infringe the constitution or the principle of unitary government.

It was authorized to visit the south and to interview anyone.

On the 22nd October 1964 the Anti-Imperialist Front, which had remained alive underground, and which contained many Communists, held an unauthorized meeting of students at the Khartoum University to protest against the Government's alleged brutal repression of the autonomist movement of the south. When the police attempted to break up the meeting they were met by a hail of stones and thirty-six police were injured. The police opened fire, killing one student and wounding others, while many members of the student protest delegation were arrested. This caused students to invade Khartoum to sack the offices of a pro-Government newspaper, and a curfew had to be imposed in the evening.

On the next day, the 23rd, there were more demonstrations, and troops had to be called in to restore order and guard buildings. That day the Umma Party issued a statement attacking the Government's economic policy and the rising cost of living and also demanding a democratic constitution. It seemed as though the forbidden political parties of 1958 had not been dissolved at all, but had merely lain dormant and were now springing up again, voicing their old cries. On the 24th the demonstrations spread to other towns, including Omdurman, Juba and Port Sudan. The Government closed Khartoum University and all schools in the affected towns.

On the 25th President Abboud appealed for order, promising an enquiry and punishment of those responsible. That evening fire was again opened on the demonstrators, three being killed. Although students had originally taken the lead, other sections of the population now joined in, especially the banned political parties, while the Communist Party, which had a strong influence on the Trade Union Federation, the United National Front (an alliance of the Umma Party, the NUP and the Islamic Parties) and some professional organizations played a large part in organizing the demonstrations. The leaders of both the Ansar and Khatmia sects called for a return to democracy and several judges and professors resigned in protest against Abboud's policies.

There was a widespread strike on the 26th October, to which support was given by some younger army officers dissatisfied with the conduct of the generals serving in the Government, and more than a little concerned for their promotion prospects. In the evening troops commanded by Major-General Abdul Rahman al-Tahir al-Makboul, the Military Governor of Kassala province, surrounded the Presidential Palace and the building in which the Supreme Council of the Armed Forces had been in session for several hours. This prompted Abboud to announce over the radio that he had dismissed the Government as a first step to political reorganization. On the following day, the 27th, Abboud said that a transitional government would be formed pending the adoption of a new constitution, but the situation remained uncertain because of differences between senior army officers.

On the 28th the staff of Radio Omdurman went on strike. The army took the station over and announced that force would be used against demonstrators. That day fire was yet again opened by soldiers, and at least 12 people were killed. This brought the army differences to a head, and the Deputy Commander-in-Chief was replaced by General Makboul. That evening, after further discussions, it was decided that a civilian government would be formed, the United National Front having come to an agreement with the armed forces, one of the essential points of which was that the south should be integrated. The emergency was to be terminated, censorship lifted and elections held, while Abboud was to remain as head of state. The strike ended, the soldiers withdrew from the streets, and the emergency finally ceased on the 7th November. About thirty-six people had been killed and over a hundred injured in these disturbances.

On the 30th October 1964 a new caretaker government was formed by al-Khatim al-Khalifa, who took the portfolios of Premier and Defence Minister. It contained representatives from each of the principal political parties, including the Communist Party, professional organizations, public servants and the universities. It also contained two southerners, one being Clement Mboro, the Deputy Governor of Darfur province, and the other Alfred Wol. Wol later resigned and was replaced by Izbone Mendiri.

Premier Khalifa almost at once had a tussle with President Abboud, who on the 8th November ordered the arrest of seven senior army officers for submitting a note to the Army High Command calling for the Sudan to co-operate with the policies of Egypt. The Premier protested that this was but a first step to dismissing all officers who had supported the 'people's revolution', but Abboud disagreed. Khalifa then ordered the arrest of seven former members of the Supreme Council and suspended the Police Commissioner and his deputy. This impasse caused riots in which demonstrators called for army purges and the trial and execution of the army junta. On the evening of the 9th soldiers of the armoured element were due to take part in a night exercise, and this immediately aroused the suspicion that a military coup was being planned. A false statement was broadcast by Radio Omdurman, purporting to come from a member of the United National Front (it was later revealed that this was a Communist trick), that the armoured columns moving out from their barracks were about to take over Khartoum, and calling on the people to rush into the streets to prevent this happening. The mob put up road blocks and generally prevented movement, despite appeals from members of the Government.

Communists and Left-wing extremists flooded on to the streets, trying to gain control of the mobs and raising the cry of 'arms for the people'. The Ansar leaders saw what was happening and in turn rushed their followers into the city in great numbers. The 'battle of the streets' in Khartoum, and elsewhere, was lost by the Communists and won by the Ansar in November 1964.

On the 10th November 1964 the United National Front called for the removal of President Abboud; on the 14th over two hundred officers petitioned the Government to purge the army; on the 15th President Abboud resigned and Major-General Mohammed al-Khawad was appointed to succeed him as Commander-in-Chief. On the 18th it was announced that a commission, composed of army officers and magistrates, was to be set up to consider purging the army; and on the 22nd Premier Khalifa decided to release all military prisoners and detainees, including Brigadiers Shenan and Abdullah. On the 3rd December a five-man Council of Sovereignty was formed in which there was one southerner, Luigi Adwok, and which replaced the dissolved Supreme Council of the Armed Forces.

Ibrahim Abboud had come on to the scene as the military dictator in 1958, after three bungling years of democratic independence. His achievements included lifting his country up from economic chaos, introducing massive industrial capital, starting ambitious hydro-electric schemes and doubling the size of the Gezira project, but he had been unable to control his officers or unite the squabbling political leaders. His failure to solve the southern problem had been the last straw. Now the older generation of army officers, educated and trained by the British, had nearly all gone, almost the last being Abboud, their attempt to govern having failed. They were replaced by a new generation of 'middle-grade' officers, who had risen in rank and matured since 1955, during the war in the south.

6 *The Round-Table Conference: March 1965*

'SANU must use all means to eject the Arabs from the South.'

SANU spokesman, 5th January 1965

Premier Khalifa turned his attention to the southern problem and through Clement Mboro tried to negotiate with southern leaders, appealing both to SANU and the Anya-Nya to suspend their anti-Government activities. Mboro wrote to William Deng and others, and nine southern politicians, three from each province, were invited to Khartoum for discussions. As a sign of good faith, on the 11th November Premier Khalifa released thirty-two southern detainees, and declared that Sundays and Christmas Day were again to be recognized as official holidays. On the 12th Clement Mboro persuaded the Anya-Nya to observe a cease fire in the south, while he carried out a fact-finding tour, but this did not last long and was never properly enforced.

After the fall of Abboud the emphasis was on conciliation, and the army in the south was told to fire only in self-defence. The new civilian Government mistakenly thought that the rebellion in the south had been directed solely against the military regime of Abboud. During this rather indefinite cease fire, many Anya-Nya visited the towns and they were allowed to move about without restriction, but they used this period of respite to recruit and to intimidate those who were collaborating with the Government. There was a considerable variation in military reaction, as in some places, literally carrying out the caretaker government's instructions, they allowed the Anya-Nya to do as they wished, but in others a harder line was taken and a few shots from the guerillas sufficed to provoke the troops into destroying huts. It was a period of immense strain for the army in the south, as the Khartoum Government was busily denouncing the evils of the former military regime, especially for its handling of the southern problem.

The Round-Table Conference: March 1965

On the 6th December 1964 the aircraft bringing back Mboro from his tour of the south was delayed, and the rumour spread amongst the crowds of southerners waiting at the Khartoum airport to greet him that he had been murdered by northerners. Up to a million southerners were employed in the north, mainly as labourers, a large proportion of whom were in Khartoum. When Mboro did not appear as expected, the southern crowds became restless and angry, stoned the airport buildings and then moved into the city, assaulting northerners, overturning cars and damaging property. In retaliation thousands of northerners armed with sticks and stones assembled, and indiscriminately attacked southerners. They also burned down the American Missionary Publishing building, suspected of sheltering southerners. Serious rioting continued all that day, throughout the night and on into the following day, the police only managing to restore order by liberal use of riot gas to disperse the crowds. On the 7th Premier Khalifa stated that nine southerners, four northerners and one Greek had been killed in these disturbances, and over four hundred injured.

Accompanied by Izbone Mendiri, on the 11th November 1964, Premier Khalifa himself began a two-day tour of the south. After his return on the 14th he announced an unconditional amnesty for all southerners who had fled the country since 1955, including those sentenced by the courts *in absentia*, and he also appealed to the exiles to return home to work for freedom and equality, and to put aside all racial, religious and political differences. He then made an offer to southern leaders that amounted to federal autonomy, but this was sharply rejected by SANU, which now wanted complete independence; indeed, on the 5th January 1965 its spokesman said that 'SANU must use all means to eject the Arabs[1] from South Sudan. Negotiations have failed; the next step is force.' But the SANU leadership was disunited. At the first SANU convention, held in Kampala in November 1964, Aggrey Jaden was elected President-General[2] and the posts of President and Secretary-General were abolished. A 'shadow cabinet' was formed in which both Oduhu and Deng were given portfolios, but neither accepted the situation. Oduhu went off to Kenya, while Deng, who had not been present at the convention, claiming to be the Secretary-General, continued to speak for the SANU in a forcible and convincing voice.

[1] Northerners were habitually referred to by southerners as 'Arabs'.
[2] According to Keith Kyle.

Two Sudanese ministers were sent to Kampala especially to meet and talk with William Deng, who had returned from Geneva when Abboud fell. They were under the impression that he was one of the most influential, if not the most influential, southern leader in exile. On the 25th December 1964 Premier Khalifa announced that an agreement had been reached with SANU, meaning with William Deng, to hold general elections in the Sudan in March 1965. Early in January 1965 Deng issued a proposal for a federal constitution for the south, which pleased the Khartoum Government but was contrary to the openly expressed SANU policy. He also demanded that the Sudan should withdraw from the Arab League, retain its membership of the OAU, introduce certain reforms, and reinstate the disbanded Equatoria Corps. A little later, on the 16th, in a letter to Premier Khalifa, he demanded a 'return to normal' in the south, the appointment of southerners to the government service and the police, and freedom for southern political leaders in the forthcoming electorial campaign. To give southerners a chance to air their views, Premier Khalifa proposed a round-table conference, to be held at Juba, the date of which was originally fixed for the 15th February 1965. At a SANU meeting at Kampala on the 20th January policy was reversed, and it was decided that negotiations should commence at Juba with the Sudanese Government. A three-man committee, consisting of Elia Lupe, Michael Wall Duay and William Deng, was formed to represent the south.

However, another southern party had appeared. The Southern Front, which had been formed in October 1964 almost immediately after the fall of Abboud, was composed mainly of southern students, government officials and employees, and it was led by Gordon Abiei. The Southern Front had produced Clement Mboro and Izbone Mendiri as ministers in the caretaker government, and Luigi Adwok as a member of the Supreme Council. It now firmly claimed to represent the south as a whole, and resented the invitation sent to SANU, but the policy of the northerners was to divide and fragment the southerners. The Southern Front reckoned itself to be a political power in the land, and produced its own newspaper, *Vigilant*, the first issue of which went out on the 23rd March 1965.

Preparations and contacts for the round-table conference were made by Professor Nazir Dafalla, Vice-Chancellor of the Khartoum University, who was chairman designate of the conference. He visited Kampala on the 11th February, only to find that Juba was un-

70

acceptable as a venue. The Anya-Nya had not heeded William Deng's call for a cease fire, and were particularly active around Juba. SANU leaders were thus reluctant to go to that town unless extra special precautions were made for their security. They were also reluctant to visit Khartoum, which the Government suggested as an alternative venue, as that city was considered to be at the mercy of the street mobs. The southerners felt that if any unpopular decision was reached the mobs would riot and so topple the Government. Back in Khartoum the Southern Front was pressing for the conference to be held in a neutral country, but the Government would not hear of this. In fact, SANU leaders were as divided on the question of the venue as they seemed to be on more important issues, and as this point could not be resolved the round-table conference had to be postponed.

In the north the internal struggle for political power continued. As there was no strong centre party, but many representatives of all parties in the Khalifa caretaker government, the highly organized Communist Party could exert undue influence on the Left-inclined members of the National Assembly. There was a continual tug-of-war between Left and Right. In January 1965, for example, the Right, that is the Umma Party, the NUP and the Islamic Charter Front, succeeded to the annoyance of the Left in terminating arrangements for arms from Algeria and Egypt to be transported across the Sudan for the use of the 'rebels' in the Congo.

Mohammed Ahmed Mahgoub,[1] Foreign Minister in the Khalifa Government, told me that he had been approached by Boumedienne of Algeria, Nasser of Egypt and Mobutu of the Congo to agree to the transport of arms, ammunition and medical supplies across the Sudan to the Congolese 'rebels', which he did without consulting the cabinet. He said to me: 'There were only between three and five plane-loads, mainly of medical supplies.' Perhaps he was prevented from allowing any more. Congolese refugees, who had fled across the border into the Sudan, were given sanctuary and put into camps either near Khartoum or in the south, established and run by Sudanese military personnel. Another tussle occurred during the first week in February over the degree of autonomy that should be offered to the south, the Left, that is the Communist Party, the Anti-Imperialist Front and the pro-Egyptian members of the National Assembly, being prepared to give more than the Right.

---

[1] Not to be confused with Abdul Khalik Mahgoub, who led the Communist Party.

Argument also arose over the date of the forthcoming elections. The Right accused the Communist Party of wanting to hold on to office. When this charge was followed by rumours that the Umma Party and others were planning to seize power by force, demonstrations began on the 6th February, in which the Communists called upon everyone to 'defend the revolution'. Once again the Ansar took to the streets. About 30,000 of them organized as a para-military body moved into Khartoum, their excuse being that they were in the capital to protect Queen Elizabeth during her state visit to the Sudan from the 8th to the 12th. A political truce during this period broke down abruptly as soon as she left.

On the 18th February Premier Khalifa resigned, but he managed to form another government, a coalition of right-wing parties and the Southern Front on the 23rd. Izbone Mendiri had to resign on the 2nd April, after being involved in an assault on a telephone official. He was replaced by Gordon Muortat, also of the Southern Front, which still had Luigi Adwok as its representative on the Supreme Council.

On the 27th February William Deng arrived in Khartoum, insisting that he was the SANU leader who had come on ahead to make arrangements for the SANU delegation to attend the round-table conference, and he was accepted as its Secretary-General. However, he was regarded with some suspicion by Foreign Minister Mahgoub, who told me that when Deng arrived in Khartoum he asked him: 'Why are your people causing all this trouble? Who are they?' To which Deng replied: 'I do not know who they are.' The impression given was that if he did not have a huge following in the south he would soon acquire one, and so he was welcomed by the Government because he was thought to be the Secretary-General, he was willing to accept federation rather than stand out for independence, and he was regarded as a 'SANU moderate' who might sway southern extremists. On the 3rd March it was announced that all northern parties agreed that the basis of the round-table conference, now to be held in Khartoum, was to be autonomy for the south, which should have its own regional assembly, while the central Government, in which there would be minority southern representation, should retain control of all matters of common interest to both north and south. The Southern Front had reversed its former demand, and accepted Khartoum as the venue.

The Government would have liked to have negotiated with William Deng only, being under the impression that he was the dominant personality in SANU, but the Southern Front intervened and insisted on being present too. When this happened the other SANU leading personalities back in Kampala refused to attend. They felt that they alone should speak for the south, and not the southern politicians in Khartoum, who had no contacts in the south and only dubious roots there. However, being under the impression that SANU was really in touch with the people of the south and had some control over the Anya-Nya, the Southern Front appealed to SANU to send its executive to Khartoum. A joint statement by all the northern political parties, the newly formed Southern Unity Party, and William Deng, speaking for SANU, appealed to SANU leaders in exile in Uganda to attend the round-table conference, which was to open on the 16th March. The Government would have welcomed a boycott of the conference by the SANU delegation, so that they could have officially recognized William Deng, and persuaded him to take something less than federation.

The era of political freedom in the Sudan encouraged the formation of more southern parties, and during the first two months of 1965 three more appeared. They were the Southern Unity Party, formed by Santino Deng, the man who had been the sole southern minister in the Abboud Governments (which did not help him gain the confidence of many southerners); the Liberal Party, revived by Stanislaus Paysama and Buth Diu; and the Southern Peace Party. The first two were small, and at this stage had little influence, and the third was simply a front for northerners. This proliferation of parties suited the Government, which sought to divide and confuse the southerners.

The round-table conference opened at Khartoum on the 16th March, and was attended by delegations from the Southern Front, SANU and representatives of the northern parties. The SANU delegation, whose leader was Elia Lupe, after much discussion was persuaded by other southerners, with difficulty, to accept William Deng as a member, but he ranked only sixth among nine delegates. As he insisted he was the leader, and spoke up as such, his position remained obscure, and in communiqués and statements the Government had to be deliberately vague about his exact status. Aggrey Jaden, the President-General of the SANU, appeared only briefly on the first day, when he made a speech antagonistic to the north. Also attending the conference were observers from seven African[1]

[1] They were from Algeria, Egypt, Ghana, Kenya, Nigeria, Tanzania and Uganda.

countries who not only listened to the proceedings but added their criticisms, suggestions and comments.

At the conference the delegations aired their views on their desired future status of the south, and put forward their proposals, which varied from outright independence to integration with complications. The southerners wanted to involve the OAU, but the Government would not agree, insisting that it was a domestic issue. Nor would it agree to hold a plebiscite in the south—thus admitting that the people would overwhelmingly vote for independence. By the 24th the conference had reached stalemate. At one stage it was nearly wrecked when news came through that a Dinka[1] police superintendent in Upper Nile province had been murdered by his Arab subordinate. Broadly, the southerners asked for self-government, or federation as an alternative, but the Government proposed only a system of regional government. When the conference terminated on the 29th no decisions had been reached, and only a few resolutions passed, which included a 'return to normal'. Southerners were to be given Government and administrative posts in the south, and greater autonomy in education, employment and religion. The result was only an interim arrangement at the best, but it was nullified by the Anya-Nya offensive in the south in July and the Government's strong counter-action.

However, a twelve-man committee was set up to carry out the resolutions, and to report on what constitutional and administrative arrangements might be possible to the next session of the round-table conference. Due to be held in three months' time, it was never, of course, convened. Six places on this committee were for northerners and six for southerners, it being the intention that, of the latter, three should go to those within the Sudan and three to those in exile. In fact, three places went to the Southern Front and the other three were taken by William Deng's section of SANU. No invitations were sent to the SANU-in-exile, and later, when one SANU-in-exile leader, Peter Akol,[2] arrived at Khartoum demanding a place on the committee, he was turned away.

William Deng stayed on in Khartoum, after the remainder of the SANU delegation had returned to Uganda, to found what amounted to another southern political party, but he retained the title of SANU

---

[1] Which gave some credence to Mahgoub's claim that the Dinkas were standing aside from the 'revolt'.

[2] According to Oliver Albino.

for it, calling his new party the 'SANU inside the Sudan', and declaring that the other had ceased to exist. Thus for some time there were two SANUS, different and differing. Deng kept in close touch with the Government, and was later formally expelled from the SANU-in-exile for 'being in the pay of Khartoum'. In August 1965, when the SANU-in-exile splintered, the title remained for William Deng to annex completely. He was now an active and recognized southern political leader in his own right, with a party of his own—the SANU.

On the 21st March 1965 the southern politicians decided not to take part in the forthcoming elections. After hesitation, the Government announced that it would hold them in the north only, and that those due in the south would take place after agreement had been reached at the round-table conference, which was, of course, in progress at the time. At first the PDP tried to enforce a boycott, but was unsuccessful, so it eventually joined in the election campaign. There was a low poll at the elections in the north, which were held from the 21st April to the 8th May, and some spasmodic violence. The results were that the Umma Party gained 75 seats and the NUP 54 seats; of the others, the Communist Party gained 11, the Beja Tribal Association (which was pro-Umma Party) 10, the Islamic Charter Front 5, the PDP 3, and Independents 15. The voting was for 173 seats out of a total of 233. Although there were no elections in the south, 21 'southern' candidates claimed their seats in the National Assembly, by default of election, and their claim was upheld by a legal decision, which tended to confuse matters later on. These included 14 Muslim merchants living in the south, who had already registered for southern constituencies.

The Khalifa Government formally resigned on the 2nd June, and a new Umma Party–NUP coalition Government was formed under Mohammed Ahmed Mahgoub, which took office on the 14th June. Sadik al-Mahdi, President of the Umma Party, co-operated with Mahgoub within the party against the Communists, because of slanderous remarks about the Prophet made by a Communist student. Rivalry existed within the Umma Party; Sadik's chief rival for power was his uncle, Imam el-Hadi al-Mahdi, who was believed to have advocated a harder line against the southern 'rebels'. The Imam desired the Sudan to become a theocracy. Premier Mahgoub wanted wide southern representation in his Government in the three ministerial seats he proposed to allocate to the south. The Southern

Front and Deng's SANU both claimed to speak solely for the south and both demanded all three, which caused the Southern Front to withdraw; consequently two of the three posts were given to Andrew Wieu and Alfred Wol, both of Deng's SANU. Mahgoub then appointed Buth Diu, of the Liberal Party, as the third southern minister, but this action caused Wieu and Wol to resign as they alleged that Diu had no following in the south. Diu was therefore the only southern minister in the Government for several months. On the Supreme Council the south was represented by Philemon Majok, who had joined the Sudan Unity Party and had replaced Luigi Adwok, who in any case had threatened to resign during the previous month unless the Government produced a satisfactory explanation of the killing of several people and the burning of houses in his home village in the south. In June 1965 the Southern Front became a formally registered political party, with Clement Mboro as its President, Gordon Muortat as its Vice-President, and Hilary Logale as its Secretary-General, and it continued to claim wide support in the south.

Meanwhile, it was a time of political confusion for the exiles in East Africa. In Uganda the SANU-in-exile was splintering, mainly because of a clashing of personalities. In June Joseph Oduhu (released from detention), Saturnino Lohure, George Kwani, Pancrasio Ocheng, Marko Rume and others broke away from it to found the Azania Liberation Front (ALF)—Azania being the name of a sixteenth-century East African empire. The remnants of SANU-in-exile were left temporarily in the hands of Aggrey Jaden. An attempt to prevent this split in SANU had been made, but failed because personalities clashed. A little later Aggrey Jaden was expelled from the remnant SANU because he was unable to rally its members in Uganda; membership was falling off as so many were leaving to join the ALF. Jaden then formed his following into the Sudan African Liberation Front (SALF). Yet another off-shoot of the SANU-in-exile at about this time was the Sudan African Freedom Fighters Union of Conservatives, but it soon faded out. However, there was a reconciliation later in the year, when the remaining members of the SANU-in-exile and the SALF were absorbed by the expanding ALF, Jaden becoming the Vice-President of the ALF. Harmony did not reign for long. In December Jaden was expelled from the ALF by President Oduhu for allegedly meeting William Deng in Nairobi and discussing the southern situation with him without Oduhu's

76

permission. The ALF claimed to be in political control of the revolt in the south and asserted that the Anya-Nya was its military arm.

It had been alleged that Premier Khalifa, under pressure from the Left, had turned the Sudan into a supply route, base and haven for the Congolese Simbas, and had also given refuge to Eritreans who were rebelling against the Ethiopian Government. For example, in June 1965, after an incident in which four former Sudanese officers were arrested, Premier Khalifa confirmed that 18 tons of arms of Czechoslovakian origin, seized by the Sudanese authorities at Khartoum Airport, had been flown in from Syria, with the approval of the Sudanese Government, for the use of Eritreans fighting against the Ethiopian Government. On the other hand, of course, the Ethiopian Government, and others, gave sanctuary to several thousand southerners fleeing from the south, and harboured dissident political groups.

As soon as he gained power, Premier Mahgoub stopped the transit of arms across the Sudan. Later he personally stressed to me that there had never been any arms sent to the Eritrean rebels, but he was at a loss to explain the Khartoum Airport consignment.

On the 26th July 1965 Premier Mahgoub began a four-day visit to Ethiopia, the object being to seal the common frontier between the two countries and to stop aid filtering through to the southern 'rebels'. On the 10th August the Sudanese Foreign Minister announced that his Government had undertaken to prohibit Eritrean refugees in the Sudan from engaging in subversive activities against the Ethiopian Government, and as a sign of good faith one of the Eritrean 'rebel' leaders was deported back into Ethiopia. Mahgoub told me that he personally discussed the issue with Haile Selassie, and it was agreed that they should not have refugee camps within fifty miles of the joint border, but the situation remained the same. Mahgoub also stated that he had evidence of Anya-Nya recruiting and training camps in Ethiopia near the border, but he said that Ato Wold, the Ethiopian Premier, had told him that if he had any evidence of such activities in the Sudanese refugee camps in Ethiopia he could immediately fly over and inspect the particular camp—a statement that not only seems to have been taken at face value but to have satisfied Mahgoub.

Early in July 1965 an ALF delegation visited Nairobi to solicit aid from President Kenyatta, and so, to counter this, in August Premier Mahgoub visited Kenya for talks. The Sudanese Minister of Information later stated that both Kenya and Tanzania had promised to crush any secessionist activity amongst the southern refugees in their respective countries, and that both the Kenyan and Tanzanian Governments desired to see a united Sudan. In the same month Premier Mahgoub complained to the American Ambassador in Khartoum that the Tschombe Government was using military aid given to it by the USA, in co-operation with the 'rebels' in the south, against his Government forces. This was denied, with the assurance that America too wanted a united Sudan. Mahgoub once told me: 'I was not happy about the behaviour of Tschombe.' The activities of the ALF were restricted in Uganda, but they continued underground, and once again President Oduhu, now the leader of the ALF, was detained by the Ugandan authorities. Premier Mahgoub seemed to be doing well on the diplomatic front.

Although it had only about 5,000[1] members, the Communist Party was becoming extremely active and influential. Premier Mahgoub, seeing the danger, waited for an opportune moment to move against it. On the 20th October 1965 seven NUP members resigned from the Mahgoub Government over the question of who should attend the next OAU conference to be held in Accra, Ghana, but a fortnight afterwards Mahgoub gained a vote of confidence which made him feel strong enough to take action against the Communists. The excuse came when a student publicly declared himself proud of being a Communist and an atheist, which caused the Umma Party, the NUP and others to demand that the Communist Party be dissolved. On the 15th the National Assembly voted in favour, and on the 17th a student burned himself to death in protest. Although the Assembly vote was held to be void on a technicality, another on the 22nd formally declared the Communist Party illegal.

Premier Mahgoub's strong coalition Government had quickly settled into office, and within a few weeks had several successes to its credit. It had gained a vote of confidence in the National Assembly, it had stopped the arms traffic across the Sudan to the Congo; it had improved relations with Ethiopia, Kenya and Uganda over the frontier and refugee problems; and it had driven the Communists underground. But on the military scene it was a different story, as the Anya-Nya had in July launched a guerilla offensive in the south which was having some success.

[1] Some sources insist that the Communist Party membership was as high as 15,000.

7 *The Anya-Nya Activities*

'The rebels will be crushed by the end of the year.'
Premier Mohammed Ahmed Mahgoub: November 1965

Despite Premier Khalifa's constant assertions that a political settlement was desirable in the south, his offer of almost federal autonomy, which was rejected, and his contacts with southern leaders, he quietly moved more troops into the south. He felt that he could rely upon the police to maintain order in the north. The army was designed for internal security tasks and not, as in many countries, for national defence. The Sudan did not visualize being attacked by any of its neighbours, because the huge distances involved would be beyond their military capability.

In July 1964, when the Congolese Simbas, led by Christopher Gbenye, revolted against the Tschombe Government, they were supported by both Egypt and Algeria, and so Khalifa's excuse for having so many soldiers in the south was that Tschombe might choose to invade the Sudan. In fact, they saturated the provinces of Upper Nile and Bahr el-Ghazal, so largely preventing guerilla activity, and even in Equatoria province—the centre and mainspring of the revolt —the heavy presence of soldiery in the towns restricted Anya-Nya operations. Under left-wing pressure the Khalifa Government turned the Sudan into a haven for the Congolese rebels.

By the end of 1964 the Anya-Nya had probably risen in strength to approximately 5,000, but only about 10 per cent had firearms. The efforts of the politicians in exile and their military leaders to obtain more from external sources failed, so the Freedom Fighters began quietly to hijack a few of the arms that were being surreptitiously transported across the Sudan for the Simbas. But the quantity obtained in this way was small. It was not until the Simbas were defeated in the Congo, when many of them escaped back across the frontier into the south, that they sold their arms to the Anya-Nya to buy food, had them stolen by the Anya-Nya or simply

79

abandoned them. In this manner several hundred automatic weapons and quantities of ammunition were obtained, thus enabling the Land Freedom Army in mid-1965 to progress from the bow and arrow stage to that of a more effective guerilla force.

When Mahgoub became Premier in June 1965 he appeared to relax the military saturation policy in the south. Many northern soldiers were withdrawn and he attempted a reconciliation policy, but his firm instructions that law and order must be restored resulted in a resumption of the war. It should be remembered that 1965 was the year of the round-table conference, when Anya-Nya operations were minimal, and both sides had been striving for a political solution. This façade was shattered suddenly in July when, on the 8th, an incident occurred between a Muslim soldier and a southerner at Juba, in which the Arab was wounded. This caused the Muslim garrison to run amok in the town; they cordoned off certain districts along the Nile bank, set fire to grass-roofed huts and shot the occupants as they emerged—many were drowned when they jumped into the river to escape. Rioting did not die down until late the following day. On the 10th there was an unsuccessful Anya-Nya reprisal attack on the army HQ at Juba. The southerners claimed that over 3,000 huts were burned, and the official northern figure of those killed was 1,019 in the two days. Juba then had an estimated population of about 40,000. On the 12th the GOC Southern Command (Major-General Sherif Habib) stated that on the 10th his soldiers opened fire on southern 'outlaws' who had attacked his HQ, and that 25 of them had been killed. The southerners alleged that this was an attempt to eliminate southern leadership. The Juba incident gave credence to persistent southern claims that discipline was poor in the northern army in the south, that the officers had little control over their men when away from the camps and garrisons, and that the men were allowed to roam into the forests killing and burning much as they liked. Mahgoub insisted this was not so and that discipline was good; he discounted reports of army excesses as missionary propaganda. Another source, a senior serving officer, told me that discipline was good and that the officers had full control over their men. He admitted that they occasionally gave them a 'free rein', but claimed that they could instantly reassert control when required. This tends to indicate the possibility of a miltiary policy of reprisal that was separate from the political policy.

The next major incident occurred at Wau, capital of the Bahr el-Ghazal province. The Southerners alleged that on the 11th July Muslim soldiers surrounded the cathedral where a marriage was taking place and, after warning four Arab soldiers who were in the congregation to leave, fired on the people as they emerged from the building, killing 75. Later on the same day a strong detachment of the Anya-Nya attacked the army camp at Wau in reprisal, but was beaten back (it being claimed by the north) with the loss of 72 killed—although on the 13th an official communiqué gave 'rebel' losses as 250 men. At both Juba and Wau a number of educated southerners had been killed, although many others had escaped. A total curfew was imposed in both Equatoria and Bahr el-Ghazal provinces.

On the 15th July 1965 the Southern Front English-language newspaper, *Vigilant*, was suspended after it gave news of the Juba and Wau incidents, and in a leading article held the Government responsible for the 'barbaric and brutal killing' at Juba, which was 'not an accident but part and parcel of a plan to depopulate the south'. The *Vigilant* alleged that there had been 1,400 casualties, with 76 killed, including 49 southern officials in the Government service, on the 8th and 9th at Wau. The southerners became alarmed by these two incidents, and on the 12th Oliver Albino, the SANU representative at Nairobi, alleged that the Government forces had killed more than 700 civilians in the south, mainly at Mide, in the Maridi District, and at Yandaru, in the Yei District. On the 13th SANU appealed to the UN to intervene in the south, to the International Red Cross to institute an immediate enquiry into 'atrocities', and on the 20th to the Secretary-General of the OAU for help, but there was little response.

Whether Premier Mahgoub's brief overt attempts at reconciliation, and to arrive at a political solution, were initially genuine or not, is beside the point; after the Wau incident, when the Anya-Nya had attacked northern soldiers, he took a tough line in the south, and July 1965 was a black month with a heavy death toll. Mahgoub stated that the guerillas must be 'subdued rather than negotiated with', and the army mounted operations against the 'rebels', burning many villages; numerous people thus made homeless fled into the forests. In particular the Muslim soldiers, as alleged by the southerners, made a point of destroying the few hospitals and medical centres in the south, to prevent the people receiving medical treatment. It was generally accepted that there were more deaths from disease and medical neglect than in action.

When Mahgoub became Premier he said[1] that he found the army in 'poor shape', with deficient equipment and poor clothing, unsuited for operations in the southern forests. On the military side he assessed the situation as 'very serious'. He defined his policy for coping with the southern problem as, first of all, curbing external assistance, then discussing ways and means of bringing the people in the south under Government control, and then reinforcing and re-equipping the army. He said that his initial military policy was one of containing the 'pockets of rebels', while he obtained more arms and equipment.

Many incidents followed, but the claims and counter-claims cannot be verified. It can only be said that many lives were lost and much hardship caused to the people, who fled in fear in such numbers as to seem to justify at least in part southern allegations that it was Government policy to depopulate the Equatoria province. In Equatoria the Anya-Nya had freedom of movement in the countryside, their camps being either deep in the forests, where it was almost impossible for Government soldiers to track them down and attack them, or in the mountain fastnesses on the borders with Uganda and Kenya. Most were within easy reach of the frontiers so they could escape over the borders should they be hard pressed.

On the 19th July 1965 the Minister of the Interior appealed to the 'rebels' to 'desist from all acts of violence' and surrender their arms under amnesty within a fortnight; forcible measures were threatened against those who failed to respond. When the amnesty ended, having produced only five doubtful 'rebels', the Sudanese armed forces were placed on full alert. After rejecting the proffered amnesty, the Anya-Nya gave the northern troops until the end of August to evacuate the south.

On the 5th August Premier Mahgoub announced that more people had been killed by 'outlaws' in the south than by Government forces, and that reports of 'several thousand casualties' were 'grossly exaggerated'; those killed at Juba numbered 100 and those at Wau 72. His Government, he continued, was not waging a religious war against the Africans of the south, but he intended to 'shoulder the responsibility for protecting life and property of every citizen, whether in the north or south'. He also promised to supply evidence

[1] In a personal interview.

of outside interference in the south. Previously, on the 28th July, the Governor of Bahr el-Ghazal province had announced that 500 persons were to be brought to trial for their part in the Wau disorders.

Premier Mahgoub's antipathy towards the southern problem was very marked and his soldiers took note of his attitude and acted accordingly. Usually, unable to hit at the elusive Anya-Nya, they made the civilian population their targets and many villages were burned, their inhabitants being scattered. On the 20th July, it was alleged, Government troops shot up Rumbek, killing several people; on the 5th August they arrived in the morning at the village of Warwajok, a few miles from Malakal, and shot 187 inhabitants to prevent them joining the 'rebels'; a little later that month they attacked a missionary station at Doleib Hill, at the junction of the White Nile and the Sobat River, and also villages near Wau and Juba. It was reported on the 6th August, on Radio Omdurman, that Government troops were attacking 'rebels' in the south, that already 16 had been killed in Bahr el-Ghazal province, and that an army operation to close the frontier with Uganda had begun. August itself was another 'black month', and (on the 1st September) the Government stated that during this month more than 500 'rebels' had been killed, while in riots at Juba and Wau another 124 southerners had been killed as well as 11 soldiers and 13 Muslim civilians.

It was not all one-sided and the Anya-Nya hit back from time to time. On the 13th August they opened fire at Katari, near Wau, killing several people, and a few days later they attacked the town of Bisellia, also near Wau, burning down the police station. That month they surrounded a detachment of about 70 soldiers near Tambura, in Equatoria province, and paratroops had to be flown from Khartoum and dropped to rescue them. The army was forming a paratroop brigade, and this was probably its first airborne operation.

Government oppression was particularly heavy in Equatoria province, where most of the devastation and terrorism occurred. The fact that the situation was not so bad in Upper Nile province was put down to a more humane Governor, who kept a stricter control over the army's activities. By the end of September 1965 it was recognized that administrative services of all types in the south had collapsed. This breakdown, together with military punitive actions, led to the spread of famine and disease; it was alleged that there were at least 60,000 cases of sleeping sickness and similar diseases untreated. Rural dispensaries had been abandoned. Southern leaders loudly claimed that the Government was pursuing a policy of genocide. Premier Mahgoub admitted that a chaotic situation existed in the south, that the police, medical, administrative and education services were not functioning, and that the Government had little control or influence away from the garrison towns. His admission was made despite his claim that the three largest tribal groups, the Dinkas, Nuer and Shilluk, were standing aside from the revolt, which was based solely on the small tribes of Equatoria province.

The missions, churches and schools in the south suffered particularly at the hands of the army, which prompted the Pope, on the 9th August 1965, to appeal to Premier Mahgoub to find a peaceful solution. Mahgoub sharply replied that he had asked the 'rebels' to lay down their arms; he suggested that if they continued to attack the southern population, it was the Pope who should appeal to the southern 'rebel' leaders for peace. The Pope persisted, and in response to a further message of protest he elicited, on the 3rd September, a reply from Sadik el-Mahdi, President of the Umma Party, that a 'group of irresponsible people, professionals and laymen' were doing all they could to turn the southern problem into a crusade, that the Sudanese Government was opposed to such an attitude as African states were 'multi-religious', and that the Pope should consider the complete Africanization of his clergy in the Sudan.

On the 25th September it was reported from the Central African Republic that the Vicar Apostolic at Wau and the Bishop of Rumbek had been killed, which immediately brought in protests from missionary organizations. On the 13th October the Church Missionary Society estimated that about half the churches in the south had been destroyed, that the majority of the personnel in the various religious orders had decamped into the forest, and that whole communities had fled from alleged 'murder, torture and wholesale destruction'. The Society's secretary in London said that it was plain that 'terrible atrocities' had been committed which, with world attention focussed on injustices in South Africa, seemed to arouse little public concern. But on the 20th October the Sudanese chargé d'affaires in London replied that 'several priests allegedly found in possession of arms' and 'rebel gangsters' had 'long been nursed and encouraged, and driven to action by Christian missionaries, and other irresponsible quarters'. He also said that 75 per cent of the southerners were animists, that 25 per cent of the remainder were Muslims, and that the terrorists equally belonged to all three groups. Mahgoub's estimates were that 90 per cent of the southerners were animists, 5 per cent were Muslim and 5 per cent were Christian.

In October 1965 the Anya-Nya attacked at Taafikia, burned the river steamer *Abu Anga,* and claimed to have defeated a company of Government troops. The army was alleged to have killed, in retaliation, all the male villagers, 89 in number, at Warwajok, previously attacked in August. With the advent of the rainy season in November military activities on both sides slackened off.

On the 8th November 1965 Premier Mahgoub was accused in the National Assembly of failing to equip the armed forces properly in the south, and of attempting to solve the southern problem by taking action against 'foreign interference'. He won a vote of confidence, and in reply announced that an extra £3 million had been spent to enable the armed forces to operate in the south. He denied any 'foreign intervention', although on the 5th August he himself had mentioned it, and he challenged his accusers to reveal any information they had on this matter.

On the 23rd November Premier Mahgoub announced that rebellion had been completely suppressed in both the Bahr el-Ghazal and Upper Nile provinces, and that it had been decided to send seven southern members of the National Assembly on a fact-finding tour of these two provinces. On the following day it was announced that Government troops had killed 100 'rebels' in an attack on a large Anya-Nya camp near Wau. Early in December Premier Mahgoub said that the situation in the south was much improved, and that 'the rebels will be crushed by the end of the year'.[1] He restated that his Government was committed to a 'peaceful solution within the framework of a unified Sudan'. However, in contradiction, the southern leaders in exile loudly boasted that 'apart from the military and some merchants, we have cleared the Arabs from the south'. An offer by President Nkrumah, of Ghana, to mediate was refused by Mahgoub on the grounds that the southern problem was an internal affair.

Despite the Sudanese Government's efforts to suppress all news of the rebellion in the south, about which at this stage little was

[1] *Time* of the 10th December 1965.

known to the outside world, reports began to emerge. Adventurous journalists made clandestine journeys, penetrating from adjacent countries, and the picture of the Anya-Nya became clearer. Its military framework was certainly taking definite form. About 15,000 Government troops had been sent to deal with the southern problem, saturating the provinces of Upper Nile and Bahr el-Ghazal, where communications were slightly better than in Equatoria. After November 1965 Anya-Nya activities amounted only to pinpricks for many months. However, in Equatoria province it was different, as the Freedom Fighters had gained a hold on the countryside.

On the 10th August 1965 a Government statement alleged that the strength of the Anya-Nya was about 8,000 'trained and equipped' men, but this is considered an over-estimate; the figure of 5,000 is probably more accurate, of whom only a small proportion were armed. Although some arms of Communist origin passing across the Sudan had been hijacked and others bought, or taken, from fleeing Simbas, the Land Freedom Army still had no motor vehicles, radios or heavy weapons, and was reported[1] to possess only one bazooka.

Resistance had yet to take on a national character. For example, the Reith, or priest-kings, of the Shilluk tribes announced their full support for the Government against the 'rebels'. While Government troops had been burning huts and carrying out reprisals on the population, the Anya-Nya had been doing likewise, and in the ruthless fighting of this pitiless guerilla war, in which neither side took prisoners, they contributed as much to civilian suffering and to creating the southern problem as did the Government troops. There was still no general sign at this stage of the Anya-Nya adopting the maxims of Mao Tse-tung, and of trying to turn the people into the friendly 'sea' in which they as 'guerilla fish' could swim.

An apt description of some of the countryside is given by journalist Anthony Carthew. He was briefed by Joseph Oduhu, President of the ALF, then doubtfully claiming to have jurisdiction over the Anya-Nya. Oduhu showed him lists of 46 villages destroyed and of 12,000 southern dead. Then Carthew made a clandestine journey into Equatoria province, marching four days to the HQ of the 'eastern group', housed in the mission buildings of St. Theresa, at Isoke, in the Dongatona mountains, near the Uganda border, which had been abandoned when the Verona Fathers were ejected months

[1] According to Anthony Carthew, writing in the *Daily Mail* of the 31st January 1966.

before. He wrote[1] that 'For mile after mile in this wilderness it is the wreck of a civilization which meets the eye: the burned-out shells of African villages put to the torch by Arab troops of the Sudanese Army. The smell of burning was always in my nostrils. It still is. Where once men worked and children played and cattle grazed, there is no sound except the coughing of the baboons and the wind rattling the dagger spikes of the thorn trees.'

The local Anya-Nya commander in this region was named as Colonel Lazzio, who was perhaps typical of other Anya-Nya commanders of this period, being energetic, flamboyant, brash and unconventional. His command consisted of about 1,000 men of all ages, some very young, in a variety of tattered uniforms, or no uniforms at all. They had only about 100 rifles. Otherwise the men were armed with spears, knives, machettes and bows and arrows. Colonel Lazzio had also enlisted a few women (apparently unusual in the Land Freedom Army) whom he described as either 'encouragers' to egg the men on to fight, or 'Freedom Fighters', who actually took their place beside the men in battle. He was desperately short of medical supplies.

At this stage the Government was still trying to build up an air force, obtaining planes and training pilots as quickly as it could, but it did not have many of either. Several bombing raids were made on Anya-Nya camps during the latter part of 1965, but little damage was done. The Government denied carrying out random bombing. Unfounded rumours were current that the Sudanese bomber aircraft were piloted by British personnel. Such aircraft as the Sudan possessed were mainly used for transport, internal communications and reconnaissance, airstrips being constructed near the towns garrisoned by northern soldiers.

Another fruitless appeal was made on the 6th January 1966 by the Minister of the Interior to the Anya-Nya to surrender with their arms. The Anya-Nya campaign continued in Equatoria province until February 1966, but at a much slower pace. In this province, where areas were dominated by the Anya-Nya, the southerners prepared for a long military struggle, while the Land Freedom Army began to establish its own administration. This led to a change of policy towards the people, who so far, to say the least, had been treated callously. Now they became important, an attempt was made to win their sympathy and to 'nationalize' the struggle. Some parts

[1] The *Daily Mail* of the 31st January 1966.

of the south had reverted to tribal authority, and yet others were 'free fire zones' in which Government troops shot at anyone they saw.

An interesting insight into this period is given by Keith Kyle[1] who spent four weeks in the Sudan in early 1966, and who was the first journalist to enter the south officially. He reported that the (then) Anya-Nya HQ was at the border town of Akobo, about seven miles from the Ethiopian frontier, in an area inhabited on both sides by the Nuer tribe, and that the part on the Ethiopian side was only 'lightly administered'; the Anya-Nya had three camps there, each containing 400–500 men. From these camps the Anya-Nya raided into the Sudan for cattle, grain, arms and recruits. Previously these camps had been badly co-ordinated, but 'a few months ago' a delegation of the ALF had descended on them to establish an overall 'regional command' under Lieutenant-Colonel Nyingeri Ajulo.

Kyle goes on to say that the real political and military HQ of the revolt was deep in the forest somewhere between Maridi and Yei, far away from army controlled roads and reached only by secret trails, where in 'mud-walled buildings clerks sit at their type-writers turning out military directives to the commanders of "regions" and "sectors", and administrative orders to the civilian "administrators" appointed to run the rural areas that are in rebel control. After they are signed, a clerk applies a neat "Anya-Nya Headquarters" rubber stamp.' He noted that the President and Vice-President of the ALF, and their two senior colleagues on the national executive were generally at this HQ, together with the second-in-command of the guerilla army, Lieutenant-Colonel William Hassan, a former 2nd lieutenant in the Sudanese Army, who deputized for Colonel Lagu when he was away, as he frequently was, organizing arms supplies in Uganda. There was, Kyle reports, considerable trans-frontier movement, without too much obstruction or difficulty, by the ALF and other top leaders of the rebellion, most of whom seemed to hover around the Ugandan towns of Arua, near the border with the Congo, Gulu, the chief northern administrative centre, and Kitgum, which controlled the 'arms trail' from Mombasa through the sparsely inhabited parts of Kenya and Uganda into Equatoria province.

Although after the round-table conference the Government at-

[1] *Across Five Frontiers:* Forum World Features of the 12th March 1966.

tempted to re-establish 'normal life' again in the south, for the army it was a return to hostilities. For example, at Maridi the Government was able to restaff its administrative HQ and fill the town with civilians, who were resettled under military protection; but they could not be allowed outside the garrison perimeter to cultivate their plots of land, the schools remained closed, and all essential supplies usually came in by air, a military aircraft flying daily between Juba and Maridi. Occasionally a military convoy was organized, but it required a heavy escort, and as all the bridges along the road had been destroyed, heavy bridging equipment had to be carried to put over rivers to enable the vehicles to cross them. The army was consolidating the towns, while the Anya-Nya was consolidating the countryside, and many of the senior Sudanese officers realized the hopelessness of trying to solve a guerilla problem with a military remedy. Major-General Ahmed el-Sharif, the GOC, told Keith Kyle:[1] 'There has got to be a political solution.'

In April 1966 Premier Mahgoub toured the south to see for himself what the situation was. He met chiefs of the major tribal groups, who asked him for arms to protect themselves against the Anya-Nya. Small numbers of rifles were issued to them on Mahgoub's authority. Also, as they asked for protection, the Premier launched a programme of 'peace villages', away from the fringes of the forests, where the people could come out of hiding and live in peace free from guerilla intimidation under the protection of the army's guns. The peace village programme was slow to get under way, and was never really a success.

On his return from the south Premier Mahgoub opened a 'Month of the South Campaign', in which he appealed for national unity. While he said that some of the 'normal services', such as the police, had resumed in the south, on the 15th May he admitted that the 'rebels' were imposing taxes and had set up their own tribunals, but he added that the security forces were there to enforce the law without terrorizing the people. Both northerners and southerners had suddenly appreciated the fact that it was necessary to appeal to the people of the south and to win them over. Mahgoub tried to urge the Government-backed tribal chiefs to do all they could to resume their authority.

A few southern leaders moved over the border into the south in 1966, but they faced a mixed reception, as the military commanders

[1] *Breakdown of Conciliation:* Forum World Features of the 12th March 1966.

did not want their autonomy encroached upon. Two of these were Joseph Oduhu and Aggrey Jaden, uneasy partners, who were leading the ALF. In the spring of 1966, in the forests of Equatoria province, Jaden attempted to form a first provisional government of the south, but he was unsuccessful, as general support was lacking, and the project was viewed doubtfully by the Anya-Nya. At this time Oduhu was under arrest in Eastern Equatoria,[1] after a difference of opinion with Saturnino Lohure. Lohure remained an important political figure, although he never led a southern movement. He threw in his lot with the Anya-Nya and was eventually killed by them[2] on the 22nd January 1967. Mahgoub described the attempt to form a provisional government in the forests as 'children playing', and he denied that it had any effect whatever on his Government's policy.

After a motion of censure, Premier Mahgoub resigned on the 25th July 1966, and was replaced by Sadik al-Mahdi, President of the Umma Party, a thirty-year-old well-educated descendant of the original nineteenth-century Mahdi, who became allied to President Azhari's NUP. His appointment caused a split in the Umma Party, as right-wing members broke away under the leadership of his rival, Imam el-Hadi al-Mahdi (Sadik's uncle), and a number of members of the Umma Party refused to serve in Sadik's Government. In fact, he was not able to sort out a government until December 1966.

Premier Sadik's approach to the southern problem was certainly different from that of his predecessor, but although he was regarded as an enlightened leader, it is doubtful whether his attitude was in any way less severe. He continued the policy of containment of the rebels and the peace village programme. On the 10th August he stated that his policy was aimed at 'crushing the rebellion, and bringing about a dialogue with those elements favouring a political solution'. A 13,000-strong army still remained in the south. Sadik, who was pro-Western in outlook, put pressure on the south to co-operate with him, and he was able to carry William Deng along with him in this respect. On the surface he was milder, and he applied some restraints on the army in the south, countermanding instructions that allowed soldiers to shoot people at random in the 'free-fire zones', destroy crops and confiscate cattle.

Elements in the army itself were not too happy about the way the war in the south was being fought, and it contained potentially

---

[1] According to Dunstan M Wai.
[2] According to Mahgoub.

discontented factions, one of which was the Soldiers and Officers Front (it is interesting to note that soldiers took precedence over officers in this secret organization). The Soldiers and Officers Front issued, in 1966, a pamphlet entitled *The Battle of the South is against Imperialism*, which attributed the killings at Juba and Wau to the troops' lack of positive motives for fighting and a spirit of despondency amongst them. The Government, which frequently ignored advice from serving officers with experience in the south, did not heed this warning that all was not well in the army, and continued to issue misleading communiqués.

Premier Sadik dismissed Buth Diu, the unpopular southern minister, from his Government, worked for elections in the south, and coined the phrase 'pacification with persuasion'. Sadik told his North African Muslim partners in the UN Economic Commission for Africa that his Government wanted to transfer to the East African group—an unusual idea for the Sudan, which thought of itself as an Arab country. Thus his statement could be taken as a gesture to the south. Sadik's rivalry with the Imam was heightened, as the Imam wanted a harder line to be taken in the south.

Meanwhile, the campaigns by both the Government troops and the Anya-Nya against each other continued, although on the 21st October 1966 Premier Sadik asserted that the rebellion was 'practically crushed' and that a charter providing a form of autonomy for the south was in preparation. That month clashes were reported in Kapoete, where the Government forces claimed to have killed 30 'outlaws'. On the 17th November the Government stated that its security forces had been in action against a 'rebel' camp in Upper Nile province, killing 82 'outlaws' for the loss of only one soldier, and that a 'large quantity of automatic weapons had been seized'. The foreign missionary associations continued their publicity efforts; on the 29th December 1966 the Verona Fathers in Rome issued a bulletin alleging that 'Arab soldiers' were continuing 'to burn villages, kill indiscriminately old men and children, and to recruit for their harems . . . the women who were not quick enough to escape', and that the Negro population of the south 'were the victims of an extermination campaign'.

The Government denied a report in the Southern Front's newspaper, *Vigilant*, alleging that on the 24th January 1967 about 40 persons had been killed in incidents in villages near Torit, and that Clement Mboro, leader of the Southern Front, had made representations to Premier Sadik about the alleged incidents. In Addis Ababa leaders of the ALF declared that 400 people had been massacred near Torit as a reprisal after an Anya-Nya attack on Government troops. Many dubious claims and allegations were made by both the Government and the Land Freedom Army, and their respective sympathizers, while many official communiqués appeared to be issued for public consumption and to boost or salve military pride. It was never possible for an independent journalist to test the accuracy of any of them.

Beginning on the 6th May 1966 a large sweeping operation was launched against a big Anya-Nya centre in Equatoria. The place was not named; there were now a dozen or so, many in remote abandoned mission stations. When it ended on the 20th the Government claimed to have killed one of the principal Anya-Nya leaders (not named) and taken 528 prisoners—an announcement obviously designed to rebut allegations that northern soldiers did not take prisoners. There were, and had been several similar operations, but few netted many prisoners, as the Anya-Nya intelligence was good; they simply moved out from their camps into the forests when Government troops approached and returned when the troops left. At times they simply moved their camps to a new site, or to a different mission station, which usually had ample buildings to accommodate the Freedom Fighters. A better relationship was formed by Mahgoub with Milton Obote, of adjacent Uganda, which led to 'joint exercises' of Sudanese and Ugandan soldiers, but these tended to be 'sweeps', which had no lasting effect and did not plug any of the gaps in the long frontier. Milton Obote had visited the Sudan in 1963, and in successive years he took part in several reconciliation attempts between the south and the north. In the forests the Government troops were frequently at a disadvantage as they did not know the local dialects and so were deprived of a good deal of essential information, while the Anya-Nya, invariably having a member of the local tribe within the ranks of the Freedom Fighters, had the immense advantage of being able to gain instant information about any Arab soldiers in the area.

Meanwhile, in September 1966, the twelve-man committee of the round-table conference reported that a centralized form of government no longer suited the country. The report was not made public, although copies were obtained by the political parties. This was not the answer Premier Sadik wanted, so he set up a constitutional draft committee to consider the problem of the south constitutionally, as he was determined that the south should remain a part of the Sudan.

The Communists in the north still strove hard for recognition and power, but on the 22nd December 1966 the High Court upheld the appeal from former Communist members of the National Assembly against the Assembly's decision (of the 22nd November 1965) to deprive them of their seats and to ban the Communist Party. On the following day, the 23rd, at an emergency session, the Assembly refused to reinstate them, and there were disturbances in the streets while the Assembly was sitting. It should be mentioned that the Communist Party was the only political organization actually in touch with the people, that knew what the people thought, felt and wanted; the other political parties were too remote, being only in touch with the small middle class and the even smaller upper class. They lacked contact with the man in the street, who was fighting while they were debating.

On the 28th December 1966 Lieutenant Hussein Osman, with other young Communist officers, tried to seize the presidential palace and the central post office but failed. He had persuaded about 300 officer cadets to take part in an 'attempt to end the state of constitutional anarchy'. About 400 people were arrested, including Lieutenant Osman, Colonel Gaafar Mohammed al-Numeiry,[1] commanding the eastern command, and several other officers. Among the Communists arrested were Abdul Khalik Mahgoub, the Secretary-General of the banned Communist Party. Although Mohammed Ahmed Mahgoub, of the Umma Party, denied that his party was involved, he too was arrested, and the left-wing newspaper, *Akhbar al-Usbu*, was banned.

On the 1st January 1967 the Minister of the Interior said that all civilians who had been arrested would be released, and later some military officers were also freed. On the 2nd President Azhari called the attempted coup 'a childish deed by a young officer', but Premier Sadik would not permit the re-establishment of the Communist Party, a decision later (on the 17th April 1967) upheld by the Supreme Council. However, following demands by sections of the crowds on

---

[1] Numeiry was released on the 9th January 1967. He was deprived of his command and sent to command the infantry school. Being told that there would be no further promotion for him simply made him a more determined revolutionary.

the streets, on the 21st January a Socialist Party was formed. Lieutenant Osman and other officers implicated in the attempted coup were sentenced to terms of imprisonment.

Relations between the Sudan and Ethiopia continued to improve on the surface. On the 26th July 1966 a joint boundary commission to demarcate the whole frontier between the two countries was announced. The next move was a state visit to the Sudan by Emperor Haile Selassie, from the 23rd to the 26th February 1967, during which both Communists and Eritrean refugees staged demonstrations, and the NUP and the Islamic Charter Front refused to take part in the reception ceremonies. According to Sudanese estimates, about 7,000 Eritrean nationalists, who demanded self-determination for Eritrea, had fled to the Sudan as the result of Ethiopian military operations against them. At the end of the state visit it was announced that both the Sudan and Ethiopia would conclude a treaty on refugees which would give them the option of repatriation or removal from the border regions. This was followed in April 1967 by a statement by the Sudanese Minister of the Interior that the Ethiopian Government had decided to evacuate all villages along the Sudanese border and to move the Eritreans living in them into new areas within reasonable reach of army and police posts. He reaffirmed that the Sudan would not interfere in the internal affairs of neighbouring countries. In practice very little changed.

There was a rather confused pattern of African countries sponsoring, illicitly or otherwise, revolutionary movements, and giving refuge to agitating exiles from other African states. For example, to the west relations between the Sudan and Chad had been mercurial over this issue, but had improved after a crisis in mid-1966, when the Chad President accused the Khartoum Government of harbouring an 'Islamic Government-in-Exile', which was alleged to be plotting against the one in Chad. There was some border friction in August 1966, when relations deteriorated, but they improved during the following month when a settlement was reached. The Sudan accepted refugees from several African countries, allowing them to live in special camps run by the army.

Elections were held in the south, beginning on the 8th March 1967. They took three weeks to complete, to allow time for the people to come to the polling stations from the remote forest areas. To help the illiterate the various parties used symbols to identify themselves, such as those of familiar animals, but there was much confusion. Despite Anya-Nya boasts they were able to prevent voting taking place in only three of the thirty-six constituencies, the three being those adjacent to the Uganda border over which the Government was not able, even temporarily, to enforce control for this purpose. These elections were boycotted by the Southern Front which, ensconced in Khartoum, had little contact with the south, so this was not a meaningful gesture. The results were 15 seats for the Umma Party, 10 for William Deng's SANU (all in Bahr el-Ghazal province), 3 for Independents (one of whom was Luigi Adwok), 2 for the Sudan Unity Party, and 1 for the Liberal Party, represented by Buth Diu. In addition there were the 21 members already seated by default in 1965. Clement Mboro alleged that the elections were not free and that the southerners did not understand them. He added that between 10,000 and 20,000 southerners had been killed by the security forces during the previous ten years.

On the 15th May 1967 Premier Sadik was defeated on a vote of confidence in the National Assembly by a coalition formed by President Azhari with Imam el-Hadi al-Mahdi, Sadik's rival. Since Sadik had southern and tribal supporters, the Imam put forward the idea of an American-type vice-president to swing votes away from Sadik. Mohammed Ahmed Mahgoub formed a Government on the 16th that contained Buth Diu, of the Liberal Party, Hilary Logale, of the Southern Front, and Alfred Wol, of SANU. Despite Mahgoub's suspicions, the Umma Party held the mistaken idea that Deng's SANU had a considerable intellectual following in the south, and decided to favour it. The SANU, under Deng, dithered between supporting federation or secession. Much later in the year, in December, the Umma Party, the NUP and the UPD merged to form the Unionist Democratic Party.

Meanwhile, the reappearance of Mahgoub as Premier brought no comfort to the southerners, who remembered his repressive measures during his former period in office as Premier. Indeed, as they feared, he reintroduced his former harsh laws and regulations which gave virtual licence to his soldiers in the south to keep order as they thought fit. He also introduced some new measures to cope with the unrest. From the Government's point of view the security situation in the south worsened during 1967.

8 Confused Southern Leadership

'The Southern revolutionary movement is plagued with
disunity and personal conflicts.'

Rolf Steiner, white mercenary

On the 10th January 1968 President Azhari officially announced that
all persons who had taken part in 'anti-Government risings' during
the previous years, including about 45,000 Sudanese who had fled
from the south, would be granted an amnesty if they returned and
gave themselves up. This was the current Government official estimate of the number of refugees, which was obviously far too low.
No refugees took advantage of this offer, and in the first quarter of
the year the now regular pattern of small guerilla operations inter-
spersed with Government reprisals continued. On the 28th April
1968 it was reported that 500 'rebels' had crossed from Ethiopia
into Upper Nile province and attacked Government security forces,
who claimed to have killed 80 of the attackers and wounded 74.
After this incident the tempo of activity slackened off for the remainder of the year, the number of incidents decreasing; for example,
for November the Government reported only eighteen 'incidents'.

Revolutionary momentum in the south was developing, but it was
moving in a confused and fumbling way because it did not yet have
a strong, clear-sighted leadership. Between 1965 and 1970 the Anya-
Nya became a recognizable guerilla force as it entered the protracted
stage of guerilla warfare, but it acted independently of the politicians who claimed authority over it, or over parts of it. Within
their own areas the regional commanders remained almost autonomous. For example, Colonel Joseph Lagu, who had become the
regional commander in Eastern Equatoria, had established his own
independent command structure, and he would not co-operate with
either the Commander-in-Chief, any of the other regional commanders, or any of the politicians.

The various southern parties and factions had differing aims and
did not collaborate with each other. The SANU, led by William

Deng, and the Sudan Unity Party, led by Philemon Majok, now both advocated a united Sudan, while the Anya-Nya in the field were openly fighting at this stage for complete independence. A compromise solution was put forward by the Southern Front, led by Clement Mboro, who was prepared to discuss federation provided the self-determination of the south was recognized, while the southern politicians in exile mostly supported either federation or independence.

In an attempt to prevent further splintering of political parties and to try to achieve unity, a number of southern leaders, in August 1967, met in the town of Angudri, in Eastern Equatoria, to form a 'Southern Freedom Government'. The structure that Aggrey Jaden had attempted to form had hardly materialized and certainly was never effective. This meeting resulted in the appearance of the Southern Sudan Provisional Government (SSPG), which was announced on the 18th August. It was headed by Aggrey Jaden, who assumed the title of President, and his deputy was Gordon Mayen. The object of the SSPG was to govern, and establish an administration, in areas under Anya-Nya control or influence, but as it lacked the support of Eastern Equatoria, the Zande region or the Moru region, its authority was not generally recognized, so its task was a difficult one from the start. Trying to ignore the dissenting and fractious southern leaders in the north, the south and in exile, it hoped it would gain prestige and strength from the fact that it was actually operating within the south as a guerilla government in the forests. Almost immediately local hostility forced the SSPG to move from Eastern Equatoria westwards to Bungu, near Yei.

The SSPG formally assumed, without any real foundation, authority over the Anya-Nya, and decreed that its Commander-in-Chief, General Tafeng, was to be directly responsible to Aggrey Jaden, the President. The name of the Land Freedom Army was changed to the Anya-Nya National Armed Forces (ANAF), but in practice the SSPG had only nominal authority over the ANAF in Central and Western Equatoria at the best, as Colonel Lagu, of the eastern region of Equatoria, still would not co-operate, and the regional commanders of the Bahr el-Ghazal and Upper Nile provinces were remote and aloof.

By the end of 1968 the strength of the ANAF had probably risen to about 10,000, of whom only about one-fifth possessed firearms of any sort, but with this increase in size came problems of desertion, indiscipline, individualism and banditry. Training camps were established and basic recruit and further training were carried out, but many of the recruits after completing their initial training did not report to the ANAF detachments to which they were posted, but instead returned to their homes with their weapons to fight tribal wars. There were also instances of ANAF platoons refusing to carry out operations, of suddenly turning upon a local rival tribe, or of merely disintegrating as they fought amongst themselves on a tribal issue. There were many cases of theft of cattle, goods and produce, of abduction of women, of deliberate arson and destruction of villages or huts if thwarted, and sometimes of the murder of people they were supposed to live amongst as guerillas and protect. Generally the ANAF fighters were not politically motivated or disciplined, and it seemed as yet that no steps were being taken to give them political training, so essential in a guerilla-type army. Central authority was weak and in parts non-effective, and all depended upon the personality, calibre and skill of the local commander, be he in charge of a region or a platoon. There were still a few extravert, flamboyant, sabre-rattling Anya-Nya commanders who had little regard for the feelings and well-being of the people, or of the cause for which they were supposed to be fighting.

In its task of establishing an administration, the SSPG took up the idea put forward by Izbone Mendiri (in 1965) of dividing the south into nine regions, under regional commissioners. Each region was to be sub-divided into districts under a district commissioner or chairman, who would be responsible to the regional commissioners. These in turn would be responsible to the combined military and political HQ which the SSPG was trying to become. The districts were organized into village councils, and an attempt was made to recruit and train home guards as a protection against the excesses of Government troops. Mendiri had already established markets in the Bari and Moru areas, both of which were under ANAF influence.

The SSPG was not a happy organization, being continually rent with quarrels and jealousies as the representatives of the smaller tribes, such as the Bari and the Laturo, resented Dinka domination. Differences arose between Aggrey Jaden, a Bari, and his deputy, Gordon Mayen, a Dinka, and friction increased as the months passed, which tended to divide further the SSPG into two warring camps. In September 1968 Aggrey Jaden openly complained that he was not being respected and supported as President of the SSPG, alleging that Camillo Dhol, a Vice-President and a Dinka, was working to depose him. Without Jaden's knowledge some of his supporters solicited ANAF support, and they managed to win General Tafeng and some of his officers over to their side to help oppose the Dinka majority in this rampant tribalistic struggle within the SSPG. The friction became such that early in 1969, alarmed for his own safety, Jaden decamped to Nairobi. Aggrey Jaden had always followed a cautious line, and he was accused of being indecisive by his own supporters, who considered that he had not taken a firm enough stand against the Dinka faction.

After the desertion of Aggrey Jaden the SSPG continued unsteadily under the leadership of Gordon Mayen, until a convention was held in March 1969, near Yei, which many of Jaden's supporters refused to attend. At this convention the south was formally renamed the Nile State, the name of the SSPG was changed to the Nile Provisional Government, and Mayen was elected its first President. The declared policy of the Nile Provisional Government, still dominated by Dinkas, was to prosecute the 'war of liberation', to fight for complete independence, and to work for southern national unity.

Having failed, after a period of scheming, to oust Gordon Mayen from the Presidency of the Nile Provisional Government, General Tafeng left it, together with a group of nine ANAF officers and six prominent civilian politicians, on the 15th September 1969, to form a splinter government of his own, which was called the Anyidi Revolutionary Government—Anyidi being an old trading post in the south. Assuming the title of President, Tafeng was shortly joined by Aggrey Jaden, returning apprehensively from exile, who became his Foreign Minister. Another prominent southern politician, who joined Tafeng's Government as the Minister of Finance and Information, was Aliaba Loboka Surur. The Anyidi Revolutionary Government was tribally motivated and had really been jolted into being because of the overwhelming Dinka dominance in the Nile Provisional Government.

At about the same time in Western Equatoria, near the Congo border in the Zande region, a Zande separatist movement, led by Michael Tawili, appeared. It was called the Sue River Revolutionary Government, and the area it claimed to govern became known as the Suer Republic. The Sue River flowed northwards from near Yambio, near the Congo frontier, passing through Wau before flowing into the Sudd. Also, at about the same time, Izbone Mendiri formed the Sudan-Azania Government in East Africa. So it can be seen that by the end of 1969 there were three governments in the south, the Nile Provisional Government, the Anyidi Revolutionary Government and the Sue River Revolutionary Government; one in exile, the Sudan-Azania Government; and three southern political parties in the north, the SANU, the Southern Front and the Sudan Unity Party; and one in exile, the Azania Liberation Front. The majority claimed sole representation of the whole of the south.

Meanwhile, elections were held in the Sudan from the 18th to the 25th April 1968. The results, not declared until the 6th May, were that the UDP gained 101 seats, the Umma (pro-Sadik) Party 38, the Umma (pro-Imam) Party 30, SANU 15, Southern Front 10, Islamic Charter Front 3, Sudan Socialist Party 2 and other local parties 6. At the election Imam el-Hadi al-Mahdi had challenged his nephew, Sadik al-Mahdi, and so split the Umma Party. The PDP boycotted the elections. There were mutterings of irregularities in the south, of bribery, coercion and corruption, and of deliberate confusion of the already bewildered illiterates who had to rely upon pictorial symbols to guide them. It was alleged that many southerners were kept in the peace villages and told how to vote before being released. Neither Santino Deng nor Buth Diu was re-elected. The Government formed by Mohammed Ahmed Mahgoub in late May 1968 was a coalition of the UDP, the Umma (pro-Imam) Party and the Southern Front. The two southern ministers were Clement Mboro and Hilary Logale, while the southerner, Jervase Yak, succeeded Philemon Majok on the Supreme Council.

On the 5th, the day before the election results were declared, William Deng, President of SANU, with six followers, was ambushed and killed on the road from Rumbek to Wau, having left Rumbek after refusing a proffered military escort. Southerners alleged that he was deliberately murdered by northern soldiers. The charge was not formally denied by the Government until over a week later, when Deng's death was first announced by Radio Omdurman, 'outlaws' being blamed for it. The SANU had made gains in Bahr el-Ghazal province; on the 7th, houses of SANU candidates were cordoned off by security forces and some were set on fire. Mahgoub is convinced that Deng was deliberately killed by the Anya-Nya as it felt that Deng had 'sold SANU down the river'. When he heard the news of Deng's death, Mahgoub sent for Alfred Wol, who was in Khartoum at the time, as he felt that Wol probably had the greatest cause to eliminate Deng. Mahgoub[1] said that he suspected him of the murder, but Wol replied: 'Not me. I am in Khartoum all the time. How could it be me?' Wol, a Dinka with an outstanding personality, had lost his seat to one of Deng's SANU candidates.

In the foreign field, during the Six-Day War of 1967, diplomatic relations were severed with America and other western countries, as the Sudan openly came out against the Israelis. A Sudanese infantry battalion was sent to the Suez Canal area, but it arrived after the war ended and was stationed at Port Fuad. During 1968 Premier Mahgoub made a break with the West, and all Americans in the Sudan were squeezed out.

At home political disturbances marked the closing week of 1968. On the 12th November demonstrations by left-wing students against the Muslim Brotherhood resulted in the death of 1 student, while 19 others were injured and many arrested; classes were suspended for three weeks. The two opposing wings of the divided Umma, that led by the Imam and the other led by Sadik al-Mahdi, composed their differences in November 1968, but no formal announcement of this was made until the 12th April 1969. The reunited Umma Party then demanded a larger number of ministerial posts in the Government than they had held before, that the Imam should be the Presidential candidate for the Sudan and Sadik the Premier, and that UDP-Umma Party coalition should continue. The UDP would not agree to these demands. They were also too much for Mahgoub,[2] who resigned on the 23rd April but said that he would stay on as caretaker premier until the two main parties came to some agreement. No progress was made before the 25th May 1969, when a military junta, headed by Colonel Numeiry, swept to power.

The period of so-called democracy between October 1964 and May 1969 was in fact one of political squabbling; in particular, the post of President was the cause of envy and controversy. It was generally agreed in principle by the major political parties that there should be a change from the British instigated form of government, by an elected parliament with both executive and legislative powers, to a Presidential one on the American pattern. The Presidency became a dazzling prize and several personalities schemed and worked to

---

[1] Told to me in a personal interview.

[2] According to Mahgoub: 'They thus seemed to consider the rule of the state a booty to be inherited and divided between them, to the exclusion of the other members of the party who did not belong to the Mahdi family.'

obtain this post. The main contenders were Azhari, who was the actual President, but without any executive power, and Sadik al-Mahdi, while lesser ones included Mohammed Ahmed Mahgoub, of the Umma Party.

9 *Numeiry to Power*

'We will not accept the Soviets as colonizers.'
Numeiry: 5th August 1971

We can now briefly and quickly trace through the seizure and consolidation of power by Gaafar Mohammed al-Numeiry, and his precarious survival, a knowledge of which is necessary as background to the struggle in the south.

On the 25th May 1969 a military junta headed by Numeiry overthrew the Mahgoub caretaker government in a bloodless coup.[1] A 'Free Officers' (sometimes referred to as a 'Young Officers') Movement had been in existence within the armed forces since 1957. A pale copy of the Egyptian model, for years it had been ineffective, but now at last it had sprung to life and its aim had come to fruition. The fourteen most senior officers in the armed forces were all out of the country at the time, either on official or private visits, so the time chosen was opportune. The coup took place at 0200 hours, and at 0600 hours Radio Omdurman broadcast a list of new ministers —it had all been well prepared. Numeiry formed a Revolutionary Council under his chairmanship, stated that he had taken power because the history of the Sudan had been 'a series of catastrophes' and because too many parties with selfish motives had been in power. He proclaimed the establishment of the 'Democratic Republic of the Sudan'. Mahgoub insisted to me that President Nasser was behind the plot to oust him.

[1] Philip Ghaboush Abbas, a former Anglican clergyman, became the leader of the General Union of Nubas (GUN) in April 1964, and by April 1969 had succeeded in bringing together five separate Negro organizations under his leadership, which claimed in total to represent four million non-Arabized Negroes in the north. These were welded into the United Sudanese African Liberation Front. Abbas claimed that he had organized a coup against Mahgoub, due to be sprung on the 29th May 1969, but that he was forestalled by Numeiry acting on the 25th. Abbas then fled the Sudan, his dream of a black power federated bloc in Central Sudan, which would eventually dominate the whole country, shattered.

103

Colonel Numeiry, who also took the portfolio of Defence, had been in command of the Khartoum garrison, and so was well placed to carry out a coup. Although he was believed to have been involved in at least three previous plots or attempted coups, so far he had not been regarded as an officer with political leanings. He had been arrested temporarily in December 1966 on the occasion of the unsuccessful Communist attempt to topple the Government of Premier Sadik al-Mahdi.

The only civilian on the Revolutionary Council was Babiker Awadalla, reputed to be an anti-American lawyer, who was appointed Premier. Awadalla had taken part in the overthrow of President Abboud and then refused the post as Premier; instead he became Chief Justice, resigning in May 1967 when his decision regarding the illegality of the Communist Party was overruled. Awadalla's Government contained only one southerner, Joseph Garang, a known member of the Communist Party, who had little contact with, or sympathy for, the south, being more of a Communist at heart than a southerner. Also in the Government were several members of the new Sudan Socialist Party, formed in January 1967 just after the Communist Party had been banned, who had extreme left-wing views.

On the following day, the 26th, Numeiry suspended the constitution, abolished the Supreme Council, the National Assembly and the Civil Service Commission, and ordered the dissolution of all political parties. The new Revolutionary Council issued a stern warning that saboteurs would be severely dealt with and that strikers would face the death penalty. On the same day Numeiry promoted himself major-general, retired 22 serving officers (mostly senior to himself), dismissed over 30, and promoted and appointed 14 selected officers to the major key posts.

Numeiry was born in 1930. His father, a porter but a minor religious dignitary, was well thought of by the Ansar, and this approval gained a nomination for his son to the Military College for the two-year pre-entry course. A good footballer and athlete, Numeiry passed and was commissioned into the army as a 2nd lieutenant in 1952. Eventually he attended the Sudanese Staff College and qualified sufficiently well to be sent on the US Command and General Staff College course at Fort Leavenworth, in America.[1] In 1966–7 he

---

[1] I was informed that the CIA report on Numeiry when he was in America included the sentence: 'If there is to be a revolution in the Sudan, this officer will lead it.'

served with some distinction in the south, after a period of command of the Infantry School.

The Government's declared policy was to work for a 'modern Sudan' and to follow a neutral policy in foreign affairs, but on the 27th Premier Awadalla stated that the Government would support 'liberation movements' and the 'Palestine Liberation Organization'. Southern politicians generally were disappointed, as his declaration seemed to indicate a leaning towards the Arab bloc and away from the African one. On the 31st May Numeiry announced that there would be no returning to 'multi-party democracy' and no opening for the 'creation of a Communist regime'; the latter part of the statement was no doubt a disappointment to many, who thought that Numeiry had strong left-wing tendencies. He also revealed that 13 officers had been dismissed and 64 former political leaders and civilians were in detention. On the following day some, including Clement Mboro and Hilary Logale, were released. Censorship was imposed and all newspapers except *Freedom* and the English language *Sudan News*, both Government owned, suspended publication. On the 2nd June several thousand people in Khartoum demonstrated in favour of the new regime.

However, discontent bubbled under the surface, and during July and August several plots to overthrow Numeiry were exposed. When he first came to power his main opponents were the Ansar and the Umma Party, so initially he wooed the Communists and gave into many of their demands. There were, for example, no Soviet military advisers in the Sudan before Numeiry opened the door for them to enter. On the 1st August 1969, in an interview for *Le Monde*, Numeiry said that his regime had 'numerous and powerful enemies', and named the Islamic Charter Front and the Ansar and Khatmia sects; in other words the traditional, the conventional and the religious. The Ansar sect, for instance, was claiming a following of over three million. Press censorship, which had been eased, was again clamped down on the 1st October.

On the 26th October Numeiry reshuffled his Government, taking the portfolio of Premier himself as well as retaining his chairmanship of the Revolutionary Council and the Defence Ministry. Awadalla, who was pro-Marxist but not a member of the Communist Party, became the deputy chairman of the Revolutionary Council. This new Government contained two southerners, Joseph Garang, the ardent Communist, and Abel Alier, a Protestant lawyer and a Dinka from Bor, in Upper Nile province. Three senior officers were arrested for anti-revolutionary activities, and on the 6th and 7th December there were further similar arrests.

In the weeks following the coup there was some sweeping nationalization of both Sudanese and foreign firms, which was interpreted as a sop to the Communists with whom Numeiry, from initial weakness, was forced to work. A corresponding further weakening of contacts with the West followed. Numeiry admitted that lack of diplomatic relations with America was having a severe effect on the economy of the Sudan.

On the 12th December 1969 Numeiry announced that a plot organized by 'imperialism' against his Government had been foiled. An American aircraft had, he claimed, landed in eastern Sudan, allegedly to prepare for the arrival of foreign accomplices of the Muslim Brotherhood. He admitted that elements of the former political parties were active underground in Khartoum and in neighbouring countries. The Khartoum newspaper, *Al Ayyam*, reported that the Defence Minister, General Khalid Hassan Abbas, to whom Numeiry had handed over this post, had said on the 13th January 1970 that the army had foiled another attempt to overthrow the Government made by an 'anti-revolutionary organization' in contact with Brigadier Abdullah Mohammed Aden, one of the officers retired after the May 1969 coup, and that he and other officers would be tried. Later, in March, *Le Monde* wrote that the tenth plot against the Government in ten months had occurred. It was the one that sparked off the Aba incident.

Tension had risen to a high point between the Numeiry Government and the Ansar, led by Imam el-Hadi al-Mahdi. During a visit by Numeiry to the Blue Nile province, to Aba Island, the traditional seat of the Ansar sect, on the 27th March 1970, an unsuccessful attempt was made to assassinate him, causing him to abandon his projected visit to the south. On the 30th he gave details of the incident. After his aircraft landed he was leaving the airfield near Kosti when the Ansar attacked the airfield with mortar and machine-gun fire. In three previous incidents he had been prevented from passing through Kosti, which was near Aba Island; about 800 demonstrators had barred him from landing on the island from a boat, so he had to give up his proposed visit as armed Ansar were waiting for him. A Government delegation, sent to Aba Island to see the Imam, was told that Numeiry must resign, which caused Numeiry to declare that the

Ansar, led by the Imam, were about to plunge the country into civil war.

After the army and police had been placed on the alert, the Minister of the Interior stated on the 30th March that an attempted coup by the Imam had been crushed after bitter fighting in Omdurman where, he said, 'counter-revolutionary pockets' had been mopped up, all 'insurrectionists had laid down their arms', and machine-guns, grenades, spears and swords had been seized in house searches. Radio Omdurman said that the insurrection had begun when the followers of the Imam had attacked and killed all members of a police patrol and four civilian bystanders. Police reinforcements were also assaulted when they arrived. Fighting in the streets of Omdurman lasted some thirty-six hours, in which 36 members of the security forces were killed together with an unknown number of 'rebels'.

On the same day, the 30th, Numeiry moved against the Ansar on Aba Island with about 4,000 troops and some armour. The Imam was thought to have some 30,000 Ansar assembled there, and an ultimatum was issued to them to surrender. Aba Island was about thirty miles long, but extremely narrow, and normally had a population of about 9,000. The ultimatum was rejected and so Numeiry's troops, supported by aircraft, attacked the Island. On the following day, the 31st, the Minister of Defence stated that it had been recaptured, that the 'rebels' had surrendered or been taken prisoner, and that quantities of arms and ammunition had been seized. Numeiry was not without foreign support. On the 30th the Governments of Egypt and Iraq expressed their willingness to come to his aid, and Libya went further by sending a token military force and some aircraft to the Sudan. On the 1st April President Nasser sent his Vice-President, Anwar Sadat, to Khartoum to reassure the rather shaken young revolutionary officers of his support.

The Imam, who asked for a period of grace to prepare himself for surrender, slipped away with several companions in two cars, but all were killed by frontier guards when attempting to cross into Ethiopia at the Kurmuk check-point on the 31st. Precise information was slow to be released, and it was not until the 3rd April that a Khartoum report announced that 'at least 120 Mahdists had been killed, for the loss of only three Government troops'. The members of the Ansar who fled to Europe later claimed that Aba Island had been attacked by 25 MiG aircraft.[1] They alleged that some had been

[1] According to Mahgoub, who wrote "At the time, the Sudan had no MiG's and no pilots who could fly them".

flown by Egyptian pilots and others by Russians, using rockets and bombs, and also that surface-to-surface missiles had been fired at them from Kosti. They further claimed that about 3,000 women and children had been killed and thousands wounded, but this was obviously inaccurate and damaged any credible case they might have had, the average independent estimate at the time being in the region of about 1,000 casualties in all.

On the 6th the Foreign Minister alleged that the plans for the Imam's insurrection had been worked out in February (1970) at a conference held at Jedda, in Saudi Arabia, where the Umma Party, the Ansar's political arm, had been charged with implementing them. He said that the struggle against the Ansar would be political, and that there would be no general offensive, but he admitted that Mohammed Salih Omar, leader of the Muslim Brotherhood, was sought by the police. Radio Omdurman announced that over 300 persons, including a number of foreigners, had been arrested, for being implicated in the plot. They included Brigadier Hamid and others, charged with having trained members of the Ansar in the use of firearms. Sadik el-Mahdi, former President of the now dissolved Umma Party, who had been under arrest since June 1969, was sent into exile in Egypt, to prevent his being elected Imam in place of his deceased uncle. Numeiry also ordered the expulsion of Abdul Khalik Mahgoub, Secretary-General of the Communist Party. On the 7th Radio Omdurman announced that all the inhabitants of Aba Island, except the 'rebels', who had either been arrested or had escaped, were amnestied.

Having dealt with the Ansar-Umma Party threat, Numeiry was faced with hostility from the Left, and especially from the Communist Party, which was the largest in any Arab country at the time; the Sudanese Government put its membership at 10,000, while the Party itself claimed to have influence over one million people. In November 1970 Numeiry dismissed three original members of the Revolutionary Council, Colonel Babiker al-Nur, Major Farouk Osman Hamadalla and Major Hashem el-Atta, as he suspected them of leaking information of Government confidential discussions to the Communist Party. Numeiry began a purge of Communists, and on the 12th February 1971 stated that he would destroy the Party. On the 24th March the Soviet Union sent a delegation to Khartoum to try to intercede on its behalf, but Numeiry was not moved. On the 17th May the Students' Federation, the Women's Organization and the Youth Organization, all Communist, were banned, and five leading Communists were banished to Kodok, in Upper Nile province. On the 25th May 1971 Numeiry announced that the Sudanese Socialist Union (SSU) was to be the country's sole permitted political party, and that a committee of twenty members, under his chairmanship, would prepare for its first congress, to be held before the end of 1971.

Suddenly, on the 19th July 1971, the Government of Numeiry was overthrown by a group of left-wing officers, led by Major Hashem al-Atta. A detachment of armour, supported by the presidential guard, surprised Numeiry and other members of the Revolutionary Council and placed them under arrest; it was all over in twenty minutes. A Beirut report stated that the leaders of this coup were really Brigadier Abdul Rahman, commander of the presidential guard, and Colonel Abdul Moneim Mohammed Riad, commander of the 3rd (and only) armoured brigade, who were soon in full control of Khartoum.

However, on the 20th, it was Major Atta who announced the formation of a seven-man Revolutionary Council, which was to be the sovereign body for the 'Democratic and Independent Republic of the Sudan'. Atta promised democracy for all popular organizations and home rule for the south; he banned all political groups set up under Numeiry, revoked all Numeiry's edicts and released fortynine political prisoners. The ban on the four Communist organizations, the Trade Union Federation, the Students' Federation, the Women's Organization and the Youth Organization, was lifted, control of the police was taken over by Khalid Ibrahim (who had been retired on the 30th March 1970), five Ministers and others were arrested and all newspapers were banned except the English language *Nile Mirror*, now edited by Joseph Garang, the southern communist.

However, there were other claimants to be the coup leaders, two of whom were Lieutenant-Colonel Babiker al-Nur and Major Osman Hamadalla, both of whom were in Britain at the time. Colonel Nur, who had been the Sudanese military attaché in Kampala until Milton Obote asked for him to be recalled because of his political activities in Uganda, said that the coup had been in preparation since February 1971, and that it had a left-wing character but was not Communist. He alleged that Numeiry ruled without consulting the Revolutionary Council. Both Nur and Hamadalla embarked on a British airliner to return to the Sudan, which as soon as it entered Libyan air space was ordered to land by the Libyan authorities. Nur and Hamadalla, in an interview for the BBC African Service, had mentioned how they would be travelling. The aircraft turned back and its captain asked permission to land at Malta, which was refused when the Maltese realized that the aircraft was still in Libyan air space, so it landed at Benina airport in Libya, where the two Sudanese officers were taken into custody. Britain later protested through diplomatic channels.

Meanwhile there was resistance to the Atta Government in the streets of Khartoum and large demonstrations occurred calling for the return of Numeiry. Consultations between the Governments at Tripoli and Cairo as to whether to back Numeiry or not ended on the 21st in favour of Numeiry, when both Libya and Egypt let it be known that they were prepared to help, and even intervene, to assist Numeiry if needed. On that day Ahmed Hamroush, editor of the Egyptian *Rose al-Youssef*, flew from Cairo to Khartoum to intercede for Numeiry's life. Possibly the only Middle Eastern Government glad to see Numeiry ousted was that of Iraq, then at loggerheads with most of the others, which instantly recognized the Atta Government, and dispatched a delegation to congratulate Atta. The aircraft carrying it exploded near Jedda, in Saudi Arabia, killing ten people and injuring six. The pilot had been denied permission to land at airports between Baghdad and Khartoum but as he was running short of fuel he was eventually given authority to land at Jedda to refuel. On coming in to land the aircraft hit some high ground about ten miles north-west of the town. There was no suspicion of sabotage. The Soviet Ambassador also hastened to congratulate Atta on his coup.

According to the Egyptian *Al Ahram*, the Atta coup had been organized by Abdul Khalik Mahgoub, Secretary-General of the Communist Party, from the Bulgarian Embassy in Khartoum, where he had sought asylum after his escape from prison at the end of June, but this was formally denied by the Bulgarian Embassy on the 24th July. *Al Ahram* also stated that Mahgoub had taken advantage of the absence of the Defence Minister and the air force commander, who were on visits to Moscow and Yugoslavia respectively; that the Atta plotters had sought to make contact with 'opportunist elements' in the armed forces, but had been joined by only part of the Khartoum garrison (the armoured brigade and the presidential guard), which had disarmed the paratroop unit in the garrison, known to be loyal to Numeiry. Other garrisons in the country remained passive, waiting to see what would happen, and did not join Atta despite his appeals.

On the 22nd the brigade of Sudanese troops serving in the Suez Canal zone were flown back to Khartoum in Libyan Anotov transport aircraft. Although they were not involved in any action or disturbances, their presence was favourable to Numeiry and detrimental to Atta. Later that day Radio Omdurman announced Numeiry's return to power, stating that forces loyal to him, led by Lieutenant Mohammed Ali Kerbassi and other officers who had refused to join Major Atta, had seized the bridges over the Nile between Khartoum and Omdurman, Radio Omdurman and the presidential palace, freed Numeiry and arrested the leaders of the coup. The bridges over the Nile were key points and so revolutionary targets; they were also a barometer of trouble, as when soldiers were seen to be guarding them there was danger in the air. Numeiry himself broadcast to the people shortly afterwards, blaming the Communists for the incident. Other reports that followed stated that Numeiry had been rescued by units which had at first supported Atta, but at this stage there was confusion. In fact, what happened was that the successful counter-coup was made by three T–55 tanks, commanded by a warrant officer with non-commissioned officers as crew, which made a frontal attack on the presidential palace. Within minutes of this assault, 32 officers loyal to Numeiry who were detained by Atta in the guest house were killed. It was not the officers who rallied and led the rescue of Numeiry, but the soldiers of the armoured regiment. Their motive was religious, as they were concerned about the grip Communism was gaining on the country to the detriment of Islam.

Major Atta immediately called for 'popular resistance to foreign interference', but he was arrested in the early hours of the 23rd. On the 25th Numeiry described in detail his two and a half days' detention in the presidential palace, and how during the final loyal attack he and Farouk Abu Eissa, his Foreign Minister, narrowly escaped death. Later Numeiry said that a total of 38 persons had been killed in the counter-coup and 119 wounded. All Soviet personnel in Khartoum were ordered to stay in their quarters.

Numeiry's vengeance was swift and deadly. On the 23rd, while there was still some firing and disturbances in progress in Khartoum, he sentenced to death, and had shot, Major Atta, Colonel Ahmed, Lieutenant-Colonel Hussein and Captain Moaweyeh Abdul Hai, whom he considered to be the coup leaders. He then ordered the arrest of all those suspected of having taken part in the coup, and all known Communists, who were immediately tried by four (later increased to six) special military courts. On the 26th Colonel Nur and Major Hamadalla, who had been handed over to him by Colonel Gaddafi of Libya, were executed, Numeiry admitting that he had asked for them to be extradited. Also hanged on the 26th was Shafei Ahmed el-Sheikh, Secretary-General of the Trade Union Federation and Vice-President of the (Communist) World Federation of Trade Unions. Sheikh was a founder-member of the Sudanese Communist Party and a member of its central committee, who had taken part in the 1964 revolution and been detained under the Abboud regime. Joseph Garang, Communist, and Minister for the South, was dismissed on the 24th, arrested on the 26th, and hanged on the 27th.

Abdul Khalik Mahgoub, Secretary-General of the Communist Party, was hanged on the 28th; Numeiry said that he had made a full confession to the effect that the coup had been planned by Mahgoub and the Central Committee of the Party during May 1971. It had been stated on the previous day, the 27th, that 12 people had been executed and that many officers had been imprisoned or dismissed. Mahgoub, a long-time member of the Communist Party, had been arrested after the unsuccessful coup of December 1966, but released on the 2nd January 1967. On coming to power in 1969 Numeiry formed a 'tactical alliance' with the Communists for expediency's sake against the Ansar, but in April 1970 he expelled Mahgoub from the Sudan. Mahgoub returned from exile in Egypt to Khartoum in late June 1970 to be placed under house arrest until detained in prison in November 1970, but he escaped on the 30th June 1971 and took refuge in the Bulgarian Embassy.

On the 26th Numeiry publicly thanked Egypt and Libya for having provided practical aid to help him crush the rebellion. He was so impressed that he said that his Government would be prepared to join the proposed Arab Federation when a single-party state had been established in the Sudan, which he thought would be in 1972. A statement issued by the Organization for Communist Action, a Marxist-Leninist group in the Lebanon, claiming to be independent of both Moscow and Peking, asserted that Major Atta's regime would not

have collapsed without the 'open interference of the three Governments of the countries of the projected Arab Federation', that is
Egypt, Syria and Libya—a view somewhat confirmed by statements
made in those three countries by ministers. On the 27th, the day the
Soviet Ambassador protested to Numeiry about the treatment of
Soviet citizens in the Sudan, Numeiry accused the Iraqi Government of being implicated in the Atta coup, but this was formally
denied in Baghdad. On the 28th, the day all diplomatic bags leaving
the Sudan were searched, it was stated that 83 officers were held for
trial and that over 1,000 civilians had been arrested.

On the 29th July 1971 Numeiry said that there was no evidence
of Soviet implication in the coup,[1] and that he did not wish for any
deterioration in relations with the Soviet Union. When asked about
the '1,800 Soviet personnel in the Sudan', he replied: 'The Soviet
experts who are here are actually here to train the army in the use
of modern equipment. They are on the verge of leaving the country
because their mission has been completed. Some left before the
events. The majority of them are military technicians, rather than
military tacticians.' On the 5th August Numeiry stated firmly that
'There is no place in the Sudan for Communism' and that 'We will not
accept the Soviets as colonizers.' The failure of the Atta coup was
generally regarded as a setback for Soviet influence in the Middle
East.

Further repressive action continued. On the 1st August censorship
was imposed, pressmen from Communist countries were prevented
from working, the Trade Union Federation, the Public Servants'
Union and the Teachers' Union were dissolved by decree, certain
East Germans were expelled, and Soviet personnel were asked to
continue to remain in their houses. Up to the 7th August some
1,400 arrests had been reported, and another 700 people were detained
on that date in the Blue Nile province. On the 15th three people who
helped Abdul Khalik Mahgoub to escape were imprisoned, on the
20th a soldier was executed and 50 officers were dismissed or retired,
and on the 2nd September 2 judges were detained and 10 others
dismissed. However, on the 10th October Numeiry released 985
detainees, including some 300 political prisoners, including Clement
Mboro, who had been sentenced to four years' imprisonment on the

---

[1] Very much later, in *Le Monde* of the 18th February 1972, he is reported as
saying that he had no proof of Soviet participation in the July 1971 coup, but that
the Kremlin was aware of it and supported it from the start.

15th July 1970 for customs offences. It was later stated (in February 1972) that of the total of 3,181 persons under arrest at the end of July 1971, only 1,521 were still in detention, and it was claimed that there had been no subversive activities during the past six months. Numeiry had ridden the Communist storm.

Once he had settled the coup, Numeiry reshuffled his Government, dismissing five ministers who had been associated with Communists or were suspected of having left-wing sympathies. Abel Alier succeeded the executed Joseph Garang, and the other new southern ministers were Luigi Adwok and Tobi Madot. Numeiry announced on the 2nd August that a plebiscite would be held in the south.

On the 13th August 1971 the Revolutionary Command Council promulgated a new provisional constitution, which included a President who would also be the Commander-in-Chief and who would hold office for six years, with executive powers similar in many respects to those of the American President. The Revolutionary Command Council and the cabinet were dissolved. Voting for the new President began on the 15th September, and when the results were announced on the 10th October it was declared that 98·6 per cent of the votes had been cast for Numeiry, who was formally sworn in as President of the Sudan on the 12th. Three Vice-Presidents were appointed, one of whom was Abel Alier, Minister for the South. On the 14th three southerners were appointed governors of the three southern provinces; they were Luigi Adwok, who became Governor of the Upper Nile province, Tobi Madot of Bahr el-Ghazal, and Hilary Logale, Governor of Equatoria province.

President Numeiry's next step was to bring to life the Sudanese Socialist Party to make the Sudan a one-party state. This was carried out in October 1971, with Major Maamoun Awad Abu Zeid as its Secretary-General. It was the only permitted political party in the Sudan. All did not go as smoothly as Numeiry hoped, and there were teething troubles within the SSP.

10 *Numeiry attacks in the South*

'There is no military solution to the rebellion in the south.'
President Numeiry, on the 1st August, 1969

Shortly after his seizure of power Numeiry made what has since become known as the June declaration. He prefaced it on the 31st May 1969 by saying that the secession of the south would be a 'crime', following on with the statement, on the 2nd June, that the south was capable of self-rule within the framework of a unified state, and within true Socialism, which was the 'simplest requirement of regional rule'. In the declaration proper, made on the 10th June, he said that his Government would grant the south local autonomy and would implement a social, economic and cultural programme for it; the programme was to be similar to the 'proposals' discussed between President Azhari and the southern leaders earlier in the year. Numeiry again stressed that there would always be a 'unified Democratic Republic of the Sudan'.

The year 1969 was one of splintering governments and factions for the south. There were varying reactions to Numeiry's June declaration. The Nile Provisional Government rejected it flatly, stating that it would continue the fight for independence. On the 24th June Fahan Utur and Ahmed Mogan, leaders of the ALF in Uganda, expressed their willingness to travel to Khartoum to discuss the proposal of autonomy; on the 22nd July Gordon Mayen, President of the Nile Provisional Government, changed his tack and said that he would be prepared to negotiate with the Numeiry Government, but that he would like the OAU to use its good offices to solve the conflict; at the end of the month, the newly formed Anyidi Revolutionary Government, headed by General Tafeng, stated that any agreement reached with Khartoum by the Nile Provisional Government would be valueless as his Government stood for complete independence. Aliaba Loboka Surur, his Minister of Information, added that his Government refused to recognize that of Gordon Mayen.

115

Apart from spasmodic guerilla incidents, there had been little real Anya-Nya activity since April 1968, the reason being, as we have seen, that the southern leadership in the field was undergoing a traumatic phase of splintering and quarrelling, and so there was no central direction. In fact, it would be almost true to say that the only incidents that occurred were ones of tribal differences and banditry. In April 1969 the largest incident admitted by the Government occurred in Bahr el-Ghazal province; it had nothing to do with the Anya-Nya, being a clash over tribal grazing rights in which some 102 people were killed and 47 wounded before the Government security forces brought the situation under control. The most notable Anya-Nya incident that month, according to Government communiqués, was when 12 'rebels' were killed in attempting to sabotage a railway line.

In late May 1969 the GOC in charge of the south stated that there had been no major actions against the 'outlaws' for many months, and claimed that the Anya-Nya had been broken and the organization dispersed into small groups. He added that most of the Anya-Nya weapons had been smuggled in from refugee camps in Uganda. However, as we have seen, the real reason for the revolutionary inactivity was not that expounded by the Sudanese GOC. Anya-Nya inactivity continued until November 1969, by which time the movement was becoming united and reactivated. In a Christmas 1969 message Joseph Garang, then Minister for the South, said: 'During the last five months we have had peace, and life is returning to normal—but of late some of the rebels have staged several attacks on convoys in eastern Equatoria, killing people and being killed.' This statement reflected the true situation in the south.

On the 1st August 1969 Numeiry said: 'There is no military solution to the rebellion in the south.' His experience as the officer in charge of restoring order in Equatoria province from November 1966 to December 1967 had brought him to this conclusion, and that was why his Government had proclaimed the right of the south to autonomy. He said that all members of the Revolutionary Command Council agreed on this course, but he again stressed that the unity of the Sudan must not be jeopardized. While showing a stern front to the Anya-Nya in the field, he made some attempt to mollify and help the population. A strict code of behaviour by his troops in the south towards the people was enforced, attention was given to improving the security of the peace villages, and in the field of community relations efforts were made to reopen medical centres and hospitals, to construct bridges and to start agricultural projects which would give work to the southerners and tempt them back to their former villages from the forests. But these measures had a slow start, and southerners generally were suspicious of and hostile towards whatever the north proposed.

Although he admitted that there was no military solution to the southern problem, Numeiry did not neglect the military side. He set about obtaining modern arms and increasing the size of his armed forces, which had been shaken by the series of violent military forays into politics and weakened by the subsequent purges of officers. Morale was not at its best, and there were factions within the officer corps. The army, inherited from the British administration, was shaped on the British pattern and had British weapons and equipment, mostly out-of-date cast-offs.

Numeiry's 'tactical liaison' with the Left caused his Government to be smiled upon by the Communist powers. The Soviet Union was eager to provide small numbers of arms and aircraft, which were to be accompanied by large numbers of advisers, instructors and technicians. The Soviet Union still regarded the Sudan as the gateway to Africa. Although the amount of military equipment eventually received was extremely small in comparison with that given to Egypt, it gave Numeiry an extra military capability which he needed to combat the Anya-Nya. It also gave him the problem of having two types of arms and equipment to cope with, British and Soviet, which destroyed the simple standardization the Sudanese armed forces had enjoyed until Numeiry came to power. Duplication in types of ammunition and spares now caused complications and made instruction more difficult. As the Soviet Union sharply limited its aid and made conditions, it has been doubted whether Numeiry was wise to fall into Soviet clutches in this respect; there were no Soviet military advisers in the Sudan before Numeiry came to power but by the end of his first year in office they numbered well over 1,000.

Early in 1966 the need for helicopters and military aircraft to cope with the southern insurrection became apparent and the Sudanese Government approached the Americans, who were hesitant and unhelpful. When diplomatic relations with the USA were broken in the following year the Sudanese sent a delegation to Moscow with a military shopping list, but it was not until August

1968 that the Sudanese Government, under Premier Mahgoub, concluded a large arms deal, reputed to be valued at between $100 million to $150 million.[1] The Sudanese were to receive T–55 tanks, armoured personnel carriers and some aircraft, but none of these items had been received by May 1969, and the few Soviet arms possessed by the armed forces had been obtained through the influence of the illegal Communist Party. However, there were still delays and more negotiations, and it was not until February 1970 that the Sudanese armed forces began to be equipped with Soviet military material. Even then the process was slow. In the interim the Sudan, impatiently, accepted some Soviet arms and Egyptian personnel from Egypt. The Egyptian assistance was mainly to the air force, and was concentrated on three main air bases, at Wadi Saidna, about 20 miles north of Khartoum, at Juna, about 30 miles to the south of the capital, and at Jebel Aulia, also south of Khartoum. From these bases, it was frequently alleged, Egyptian, and later Soviet, pilots flew operational sorties to the south.

During 1969 the Sudan possessed an army of about 26,500 men,[2] formed into four infantry brigades of four battalions each, three independent infantry battalions, one armoured regiment, a paratroop regiment and three artillery regiments. Manpower of this voluntary force had increased only slowly, considering the potential and the size of the southern problem. At the end of 1969 the Sudanese armed forces still had their original British material, which amounted to 50 Saladins, 60 Ferrets and 45 Commandos (all being armoured cars), about 50 25-pounder field guns, 40 105 mm. howitzers, 20 120 mm. mortars and 80 Bofors 44 mm. guns, while as regards aircraft they had 5 BAC–145T, Mark Vs, 11 Provosts, 3 Pembrokes and 3 F–27 Troopships. To this inventory by the end of 1969 had been added some (number never specified by any source) 85 mm. Soviet anti-aircraft guns, 16 MiG–21s and 5 Anotov–24 transport aircraft. These brought the Sudanese air force up to a strength of about 32 combat planes, piloted and serviced by about 450 personnel. The 50 Saladins and 6 of the Provosts were reputed to have been promised as a good-will gesture during the British royal visit to the Sudan in February 1965, without proper Government consulta-

---

[1] The Russians eventually took the Sudan's cotton crop in a barter exchange for the armaments, and later sold it on the world market at a great profit, an unexpectedly capitalistic act by a Communist power, that upset the Sudanese.

[2] According to Adelphi Paper No. 67, of May 1970.

tion, and had been pushed through on the insistence of the British Foreign Office. In addition 12 field radio sets of a type on trial, but not in service with the British army, were sent, as communications in the Sudanese armed forces were extremely poor, resting mainly upon the telegraph system established by Lord Kitchener in the early years of the century. Of these 12 sets, I was told, only two worked, but the Sudanese, thinking themselves at fault technically, were too proud to admit the failures. This type of radio set was not adopted for use in the British army.

During the following eighteen months to two years, that is to the end of 1971, more Soviet equipment arrived, making the total up to at least 30 T–34s, 60 T–54s, 50 T–56s and some T–59s (all tanks), plus some Soviet BTR–40s and BTR–152s (light armoured vehicles) and some more (again an unspecified number) 85 mm. anti-aircraft guns. During this period the army strength was increased by about 10,000, to 36,000, three anti-aircraft regiments having been formed, and the infantry brigades having been increased in number to six, one of which served on a rotation basis in the Suez Canal Zone. The border police amounted to about 10,000 men. The strength of the air force had increased to over 700, and its combat aircraft to over 40 (that still included the original 16 MiG–21s), to which had been added 8 MiG–17s and at least 8 Mi–8 helicopters. The soldiers' uniforms, being mainly of the old British tropical pattern of khaki drill, with shorts and bush hat, originally designed for desert warfare, were most unsuitable for fighting in the forests, and so Numeiry clothed his soldiers in green. The beret was adopted as the headdress.

A staff college had been set up by British officers in August 1963, with the aim of its being 'Sudanized' by 1967. The bulk of the instruction and the discussions were in English, the object being to give a general staff training to colonels and lieutenant-colonels, and to bring less senior officers up to the standard required to attend the British staff college, which some Sudanese officers were later able to do. A children's school at Omdurman was converted for the purpose. The senior British officer noted that the Sudanese army (in 1963–4) was still organized on British lines, and was using old British equipment, except for some (unspecified) West German equipment. He found that it was working from ten-year-old British military training pamphlets, used in the days of the old Sudan Defence Force, and that there had been no 'collective training' for 'some years'. This officer was able to tour the south where military operations were in progress against the 'local dissident tribes and remnants of the 1955 mutineers', and this first-hand knowledge of conditions there proved useful to him in setting internal security exercises for the students on subsequent courses. He claimed that there was a high standard of morale and discipline in the Sudanese armed forces, and that the staff course in session continued throughout the disturbances leading to the fall of President Abboud.

The British eventually left in 1967, and the Sudanese themselves ran the staff college until Numeiry brought in Russian advisers. Soon there was a large Soviet military mission, headed by a major-general, which organized all training, including that at the staff college, and also controlled the Soviet advisers, who were distributed out to formations right down to unit level. A seven-man Soviet team took over the staff college, and immediately imposed the Soviet doctrine of massive manpower, massive fire-power and tactics on the students. The teaching and discussions went over the heads of the students, whose army at the time possessed less than 50 tanks, leaving them bewildered. The Soviet instructors were inflexible, and unable to modify their teaching or tactics to local conditions. Soviet tactics required a greater ratio of officers than the Sudanese armed forces possessed, and so more had to be hastily commissioned. Commands were detailed to send in a quota of candidates, which caused the selection process to be poor and allowed nepotism to creep in. The syllabus at the military college was also poor and unimaginative, and an unduly large proportion of the time was spent on drill. The quality of the officer cadre, especially the younger element, dropped.

After the Atta coup in July 1971 over 200 young officers were dismissed. This left a gap which Numeiry filled by promoting non-commissioned officers to be officer-cadets, and sending them to the military college, where they were put through a special course. Those who did not pass, usually because of lower educational standards, were given another chance, and some a third. In this way Numeiry gained a hard core of junior officers loyal to himself, and who owed their status and promotion to him, which was a good counter-balance to other factions within the army. The Sudan did not as a rule send officer-cadets to Sandhurst, because initially it could not afford to do so, and so it had perforce to establish its own military college, which took in officer-cadets from other countries, mainly African, such as from Uganda. This meant that the Sudanese officers lacked breadth of experience and tended to be parochially minded. In September 1971, after the Atta coup and the expulsion of Soviet advisers, the British came back briefly to run the staff college.

Generally, the Soviet attempt to teach and impose their military doctrines of massive might on the tiny Sudanese army had been a failure and had damaged its efficiency. The Russians persistently intermixed politics with training, which grated on the ears of the religious-minded Sudanese.

For example, pilot-training for the MiGs took place in the Soviet Union, and was a two-year course. As the trainees had first of all to acquire a working knowledge of Russian, the time-lag in producing trained pilots was a long one. Included in this course were thick wads of political training, which the Sudanese had to sit through as well, and which they considered to be both time-wasting and irrelevant, but the Russians remained inflexible.

Although Numeiry's offensive against the Anya-Nya in the south did not commence until November 1969, the first action of note connected with it occurred in the September, when Radio Omdurman reported that in a clash at Pibor, in Upper Nile province, 87 'outlaws' were killed and large quantities of arms seized. During December 1969 there were Government attacks on two Anya-Nya bases in eastern Equatoria, one near Torit and the other near Kaya. According to the *New York Times* of the 2nd January 1970, '40 to 50 Government troops were killed in the town of Torit, within the last few weeks in a battle of unusual size', but it seems that there was stiff fighting at the outpost of Kaya, which was destroyed. The *Christian Monitor*, of the 14th January 1970 claimed that the army during 1969 had massacred entire villages, or segments of their population, in at least 212 cases. The paper quoted alleged instances, such as one at Marial Aguog, in Bahr el-Ghazal province, where all 700 inhabitants were alleged to have been machine-gunned, and another at the police post at Ulang, south of Nasir, Upper Nile province, where 2,000 people were killed and their cattle driven off northwards.

On the 20th December 1969 the north made a bombing raid in the south, using three MiGs, on the town of Nyerol, in Upper Nile province, in which a cattle camp was hit and allegedly 'several thousand' cattle killed. After this the air force, with its Soviet aircraft, came increasingly into action, bombing, machine-gunning and firing rockets, while in ground attacks Soviet-built helicopters closely supported the troops, and were frequently used to lift them forward, to surround villages suddenly, to assault Anya-Nya camps or to block escape routes.

Rumours soon spread that many of the aircraft were flown by Egyptian, and even Russian, pilots. The truth is hard to determine, although both Egypt and the Soviet Union consistently denied that any of their personnel were involved in operations in the south. It should be remembered that the period from May 1969 until July 1971 was that of Numeiry's 'tactical alliance' with the Left, so one can presume that such help was available if Numeiry needed it—which he did. As the first Soviet-trained pilots did not return to the Sudan until the spring of 1970 there may have been some substance in the allegations by supposition alone, as no foreign mercenary pilots were hired by Numeiry. Again, Soviet personnel may have flown as co-pilots with the Sudanese until they gained sufficient experience. Early in 1971 the Anya-Nya were claiming that the north was using 25 Soviet-built aircraft to bombard the south. By mid-1971 Sudanese pilots were flying all Numeiry's aircraft, but by then the aerial offensive had tended to die down. Later, Colonel Lagu stated that the last MiG to fire rockets into his HQ at Morta, in Eastern Equatoria, had done so in July 1971, since when he had seen only a few Anotovs on reconnaissance patrols.

Both Soviet and Egyptian personnel were in the north in a training role and as advisers and technicians. Also, although this is formally denied by both countries, Egyptian and Soviet personnel were in the south as observers, and perhaps also as advisers. Several Western correspondents reported evidence of a Soviet presence in the south, and Colonel Lagu later alleged Soviet participation, claiming that bodies found in an aircraft brought down by the Anya-Nya had been identified as Soviet by dental evidence.

There were many allegations of Government bombing by the south. In November 1970 there was a report alleging that 800 people had been killed in this way, but it was vaguely worded and the location was difficult to determine. It was again denied that any Soviet or Egyptian pilots were flying Sudanese aircraft on missions to the south, and by this time the denial was probably correct, as Sudanese pilots had taken over, but they may still have had foreign co-pilots. The Government insisted that there was no random bombing, and that aerial action was only taken against Anya-Nya camps when they were located. In February 1971 it was alleged that a Government bombing raid on an Anya-Nya base near Morta, near the Uganda border, caused 1,000 civilian casualties.

In April 1970 the Government stated that some of the villages in the south had to be 'protected' by northern troops against the 'outlaws', but many of the inhabitants were still in the forests, frightened to return to their homes. The number of southern refugees registered with the UN High Commissioner for Refugees that month was 145,000, a figure that rose to 176,000 by September.[1]

In May 1970 Government security forces were reported to have captured 502 'rebels' and quantities of arms of British, West German and Israeli origin, but at the end of July the Anya-Nya again attacked the rebuilt police post at Kaya, near Torit. Complaints and allegations poured out against the activities of the Government troops in the south. On the 26th July 1970 in an incident at Banja, on the Sudan–Zaire border, a church was reported set on fire and 27 people burnt to death inside it, in all 44 people being killed, but the north ridiculed this allegation. In August the southerners alleged that 'returned refugees' were put into 'peace villages' under supervision, and that later the bodies of some, shot in the back of the head, were seen floating down the Nile. Between July and September 1970 alleged incidents committed by Government forces included 11 villages burned in one day in the Juba district, in which 11 people were killed; later, 77 were killed in other villages and several tortured, and 34 were killed at a funeral. Many of the allegations, including some from missionary sources, tended to be vague and confusing, omitting dates and locations, and it was suspected that incidents and casualties were exaggerated.

Of interest, in the absence of confirmed precise detail, is the Anya-Nya report from the Upper Nile region (presumably approved by Colonel Akwon although signed by Stephen Ciec Lam, the former Minister of Information in the Nile Provisional Government), sent to the editor of the *Grass Curtain* and obviously intended for publication, listing the actions during the period from August to December 1970. It claims that on the 25th August the ANAF attacked the Arab district HQ at Akobo, killing 16 northerners and losing one man themselves, and that on the 27th the ANAF attacked the district

[1]Broken down as 59,000 in the Congo; 20,000 in Ethiopia; 72,000 in Uganda; and 25,000 in the Central African Republic. No figures were available for Chad and Kenya.

HQ at Nasir and occupied the town for twenty-four hours, killing 24 Arab soldiers but losing one captain themselves. On the 11th October, the report states, a station at Burmah, 30 miles from Akobo, manned by two platoons of Government troops, was attacked by the ANAF, who overran it, killing 102 Arabs—of whom 40 were killed when a truck they were riding in hit a mine—for the loss of 7 ANAF killed and 17 wounded. Reinforcements sent from Akobo were included among the dead, while the ANAF captured 22 automatic weapons, 15 of them Soviet-made.

Another incident quoted in the report stated that on the 30th November the Government post at Keir, 40 miles from Nasir, manned by two platoons, was attacked and overrun by the ANAF, 4 Arabs with their arms being captured, while ANAF casualties were not stated. That was an example of the pattern of Anya-Nya regional activity, as the Anya-Nya liked it to be known, which was repeated in the other regions.

This particular report ended with the information that on the 1st December 1970 the station at Pachola, in Pibor district, manned by a company of troops, was attacked by the ANAF, and that three-quarters of the town was occupied. No other details were given, perhaps because a report from the commander of the final Pochala operation to Upper Nile HQ, by the Anya-Nya commander concerned (who is not named) was published in the same issue of the *Grass Curtain*. There is a discrepancy in the dates of six weeks, but it undoubtedly relates to the same incident. According to the operational commander, who had 118 men, he opened the attack on Pachola, held by 300 soldiers and 150 police, at midnight on the 5th January 1971 with a preliminary mortar barrage, after which there was hand-to-hand fighting, the operation lasting, in all, eleven hours. The ANAF claimed to have killed 157 men, captured 2, and seized 78 automatic weapons and 26,000 rounds of ammunition, for the loss of 11 killed and 21 wounded. They then burned the Pachola post to the ground, destroyed two armoured cars, guns in vehicles that could not be taken away, two vehicles and telephone communication equipment. This was the first such attack of its kind in Upper Nile province, and was regarded by the ANAF as one of its best fought battles, but it resulted in an alleged reprisal massacre of the civilian population of Pachola, in which at least 180 people were killed. The date was not mentioned and is uncertain.

One Government action on which slightly more detail is available is the northern attack on the HQ of the central region of Equatoria, at Morta, in September 1970. Northern troops moved out in trucks by road from Yei to establish a base camp on the road just to the north of Morta, near the village of Bori, but the Anya-Nya immediately mined the road and, they claimed, destroyed 5 trucks. The road being unsafe, from the 19th onwards, other soldiers were ferried to Bori by helicopter until the strength of the attacking force exceeded 3,000, a whole brigade being used for the operation.

On the 24th the troops advanced on Morta under the cover of artillery fire and supported by three MiGs and an Anotov aircraft, bombing and firing rockets, but the Anya-Nya stood their ground and the assault was repulsed, the ANAF claiming that in the evening two trucks laden with dead returned to Yei. On the next day, the 25th, the Government force renewed its attack, with increased air and artillery support, but again the assault was held. On this day the Anya-Nya claimed to have brought down one helicopter. A third assault was launched on the 26th and was again held.

The attacking force, with its overwhelming superiority in fire power and air cover, had expected the Anya-Nya to fade away into the forests after nominal resistance—an 'exercise with live ammunition' in which the Anya-Nya would disperse 'according to plan'. In other words, normal guerilla tactics, which the Anya-Nya had practised so often before—but this time they had not done so. The plan of attack had to be changed, and the troops were lifted by helicopter into an advantageous position on some high ground, which they would not have been able to reach on foot, and which was actually behind the rough Anya-Nya holding-line. During the following week there was little ground activity, but plenty of aerial action against the Anya-Nya group holding out, while the Arab position on the high ground was steadily reinforced until the remainder of the brigade had been moved there. On the last day of the month[1] another helicopter was brought down by the defenders,[2] who also claimed to have hit a plane with machine-gun fire, and which was last seen making for Juba. Later reports from Juba confirmed that a MiG had crashed about two miles from the town. On the 1st October the Government forces behind the Anya-Nya lines moved into the assault, hitting the Freedom Fighters, whose positions were facing the other

[1] The actual report quotes the '31 [*sic*] September 70'.
[2] It was claimed that two of the dead were Russians, identified by dental evidence.

direction, in the rear; they do not seem to have appreciated the new threat. After some resistance the Anya-Nya faded away into the forest, having held up about 3,000 soldiers for nearly a fortnight. The ANAF claimed that the fighting for Morta had extended to twenty-five days, but their sense of time was always doubtful.

On the 8th November 1970 the Defence Minister, General Khalid Hassan Abbas, announced that 'four rebel bases have been destroyed', without giving their locations. In November an announcement that the Presidents of Egypt, Libya and the Sudan intended to create a federation between their countries caused alarm and apprehension in the south, partly because such a federation might open wide the door to Egyptian and Libyan military intervention in the south, and partly because it was another sign that Numeiry was associating himself with the Arabs and not the Africans.

Since the Six-Day War of 1967 rumours had been in existence of Israeli intervention in the south and Israeli aid to the Anya-Nya. These were reinforced by the Government's allegations that the Israelis were supplying arms to the 'rebels'. In particular it was asserted that an unmarked DC aircraft, flown by night from either Ethiopia or Uganda, dropped Soviet-made arms, captured by the Israelis in the June War, on Owiny Ki-Bul, the HQ of the eastern Equatoria region. The expression Owiny Ki-Bul is generally taken to be the war cry of the Acholi tribe (which spreads into Uganda), meaning 'hear the drums'. The place of that name is about ten miles inside Equatoria from the Uganda border, and was at times the GHQ of the Anya-Nya. However, it became the practice to refer to GHQ itself as 'Owiny Ki-Bul', wherever it happened to be. Of course, it moved several times. Certainly Soviet arms appeared in small numbers in the hands of the Anya-Nya during 1969 and 1970, but whether they came into the south in this manner, or were simply smuggled over the frontiers of adjacent countries, was neither proved nor disproved. There were also loud allegations that the Israelis were running training camps in Ethiopia and Uganda for the Anya-Nya, near the Sudanese border, and giving other clandestine aid, but while supposition and deep suspicion existed there was little real evidence.

There had been contact between Uganda and Israel for some years. In 1962 President Milton Obote visited Israel, and Golda Meir, then Israeli Foreign Minister, returned the visit the next year. In 1966 Premier Eshkol went to Uganda. After the June War of 1967 the

126

Israelis made a more determined effort to gain influence with certain African states, diplomatically and by giving expertise and technical aid, with the object of neutralizing sympathy for the Arab countries in the north. The Israelis managed to establish military training missions in Ethiopia, Zaire and Uganda. As the Israelis were training the Ethiopian police and sections of the Ethiopian armed forces, the opportunity to help the southerners materially was there.

In 1968 General Idi Amin, the Ugandan Inspector-General, had visited Israel, seen the Israeli Independence Day Parade, been awarded the Israeli parachute badge, and had come away impressed and favourably inclined towards their cause. The Israelis were hoping to use Uganda as a base for giving active aid to the ANAF, but they had limited success. In 1970 Milton Obote was moving much closer towards Numeiry, and when in that year an Israeli general[1] visited Uganda to ask for overflying permission, for aircraft refuelling facilities at either Entebbe or Gulu, and for facilities to train guerillas in north Uganda, he was refused. This request certainly gave colour to the Khartoum Government's allegations.

In late January 1971 General Amin seized power in Uganda, ousting Milton Obote, who sought refuge in Tanzania. Amin ejected the Soviet training mission that was operating in Uganda and brought in an Israeli one to train his air force so another opportunity to help the ANAF presented itself to the Israelis. Prior to his coup General Amin had been in contact with the Anya-Nya, and is said to have secretly visited Colonel Lagu at his HQ in the south, accompanied by two Israeli officers, on at least two occasions, and to have assisted the ANAF by allowing supplies to them to cross the Uganda border. Later, when Obote cooled off towards the south, Amin was said on occasions to have ordered Ugandan officers on the frontier to allow supplies for the Anya-Nya to pass. It was further reported that he switched medical supplies consigned for the Ugandan army to the ANAF. According to one source[2] Obote is said to have been aware of this in late 1970, but he does not seem to have taken any action.

For months before his coup Amin had been recruiting 500 southerners to help him overthrow Obote. Soon afterwards he had about 1,500 in his Ugandan army, a number that was increased later to 3,000. Towards the end of 1971 Amin fell under the influence of Colonel Gadaffi, of Libya, and veered over to the Muslim Arab

---

[1] According to *Amin* by David Martin.
[2] According to David Martin.

camp and away from that of the Israelis, so if indeed the Israelis had been sending arms and supplies to the south and helping to train the Freedom Fighters from Uganda (and there were strong indications that they were doing this), the opportunity melted away after several months under the Amin regime.

Rolf Steiner, the German white mercenary, who was in the south for a while, later alleged at his trial that the Israelis had bases in the south, in Ethiopia and Uganda, some as close as eight miles from the Sudanese border. The Israelis, he said, had established a military school actually in the south, and had taken part in laying mines in rivers.[1] He asserted too that President Numeiry actively helped Milton Obote, allowing him, early in 1971, to recruit an armed force and to train it in the camp at Owiny Ki-Bul. This was the real Owiny Ki-Bul captured by the northern troops on the 25th January 1971 which had been evacuated when attacked as it was in open country; the GHQ of the ANAF then moved into the Immatong Mountains. Guarded by a detachment of Arab soldiers, Owiny Ki-Bul, near Issore, a grass-roofed hut encampment, housed an armed cadre of Ugandans hostile to General Amin. In August 1971 a Ugandan reconnaissance plane flew low over the camp at Owiny Ki-Bul, and when fired at from the ground took evasive action and disappeared; it was believed to have President Amin as a passenger. In December 1971 the Khartoum Government warned Obote that he must move his armed force, then about 200 armed men, out of the south, and it finally left in March 1972.

Apart from the possible Israeli help, so far the south had fought alone. There was no suggestion of military allies or mercenary soldiers until on to the southern scene came Rolf Steiner, a white mercenary, fresh from his exploits in the recent wars in the Congo and Biafra, and whose trial in Khartoum in 1971 was given world-wide publicity. Steiner made hardly any impact on the south, which in general seemed embarrassed by his presence, but in view of his experience some of his comments on the war in the south are interesting.

Born in 1931 in Germany, Steiner belonged to the Hitler Youth and the Nazi Storm Troops. He joined the French Foreign Legion

---

[1] Later, in April 1972, President Amin expelled all Israeli diplomats, advisers and technicians, who numbered about 700—but that was after the cease fire in the south. The Israelis stated that there were only 149 working in Uganda, plus 321 dependants.

after World War II and saw action in Indo-China and Algeria before becoming a white mercenary in Africa. He gave evidence at his trial that he first visited the south in July 1969 to discuss the situation and to help build a radio station and an airport. His services were rejected by the ANAF, so he attached himself to General Tafeng in November 1969 and was appointed, with the rank of colonel (later major-general), to raise and command an army of between 20,000 and 24,000 men for Tafeng's newly formed Anyidi Revolutionary Government. He was unable to recruit the required army because of dissension between the southern groups. He applied for 'citizenship' of the Republic of Anyidi. When the Anyidi Revolutionary Government ceased to exist in April 1970 he was again rebuffed by the now uniting Anya-Nya. Steiner denied that he had ever commanded, or even collaborated, with the Anya-Nya, which was probably true, but he admitted his involvement with the 'self-styled General and President of the Anyidi Republic', which was true. He boasted of gaining the confidence of the 'rebel' leaders, but this claim was dubious, as he could only have meant the Anyidi personalities.

After a period of wandering restlessly about the south, unsuccessfully offering his services, in early November he crossed over into Uganda, presumably with the intention of travelling to Europe, but he was immediately arrested in Kampala—on the 11th November—and kept in detention for three months while President Milton Obote decided whether he should be handed over to the Sudanese Government. Obote later said that he had declined a West German request for Steiner's extradition, but eventually he agreed to comply with an OAU ruling, which as a body had sharp views on the employment of white mercenaries in Africa, and Steiner was handed over to the Sudanese on the 10th January 1971. A fortnight later Obote was overthrown by Amin. On the 18th Steiner was presented at a press conference in Khartoum, at which the Secretary-General of the OAU expressed the hope that 'this was the beginning of the end of the white mercenary activities in Africa'. Certainly Steiner was the first to be arrested and brought to trial.

Steiner's trial opened in Khartoum on the 5th August and lasted until the 12th September. Although charged on numerous counts, he was only found guilty of inciting war against the Government, illegal entry into the Sudan and distributing medical drugs, for which he was sentenced to death, a sentence which was commuted to twenty years' imprisonment by President Numeiry.

Steiner was something of a psychopath. He claimed to have helped in teaching farming, and said that he thought of the rebellion as a means to exert pressure on the north to obtain a peaceful settlement. He gave a long statement to the court in which he made some fairly improbable accusations that involved the British, the American Government, the US Central Intelligence Agency, the US Peace Corps and the Israelis. He kept a frank diary, extracts of which were read in court. One witness was Brigadier Khalifa Karrar, who claimed to have led a raid on an Anya-Nya camp in 1970, where Steiner was said to be at the time, while another, ex-President Milton Obote, declined to give evidence, asserting that his life would be in danger.

Steiner argued that the whole southern revolutionary movement was plagued by disunity, personal conflicts and lack of both military and political co-ordination. Of the southern guerillas he said that they fought very well against each other but against the 'Arabs' they felt inferior. After several months' training at 'Anya-Nya camps' many deserted with their arms, preferring to fight in their own tribal areas under their local, self-appointed colonels. They were never happy or confident away from their own localities, and several of his own carefully planned attacks ended in confusion with one or more of the 'resistance platoons' fighting its own private war, losing its own war, or simply not fighting at all.

Concurrently, with his military offensive, President Numeiry continued his community programme to help the people in the south and to try to win them over to his side. He began by making efforts to improve communications by building and repairing roads and bridges, but there was a shortage of money available for this purpose, and it was not until after Numeiry went on a state visit to China (from the 6th–13th August 1971) that the Chinese Government made him loans that enabled this programme to be started— but it made slow progress. By April 1970, in his attempt to reclaim deserted agricultural land, he had opened about forty resettlement areas in Equatoria. In April 1971 Joseph Garang, then Minister for the South, claimed that progress had been made in this field, quoting the examples of a large rice-growing project at Aweil, in the Bahr el-Ghazal province, a jute scheme at Tonj, a tomato farm at Wau, and the bringing back into use of the coffee farms at Maridi, Oba, Matika and Kargulla.

There was a dearth of medical facilities in the south. Garang also claimed some improvement in this sphere. A sixty-bed hospital had been completed at Gogreal, in Bahr el-Ghazal province, health and dental centres opened at Wau, an eye clinic opened at Malakal, the hospital at Wau improved, hospitals at Nasir and Doro reopened, a hospital at Kodok was under construction, and a school for medical assistants had been opened at Juba. In general the Government had some success in the population centres that were protected by troops, but absolutely none in the countryside.

11 *Lagu Unites the South*

'The Khartoum Authorities are using the southern problem
as a market commodity to solicit aid for the development of
the north and the subjugation of the south.'
Colonel Joseph Lagu, Commander, Anya-Nya, 1970

At last out of the morass of quarrelling southern personalities one
rose to tower above all the others: he was Joseph Lagu, who had
become the Commander of the Eastern Equatoria Region, and whose
name soon became synonymous with the military struggle of the
south. Born in Equatoria, of the Madi tribe, on the 21st
November 1931 at the village of Moli, about eighty miles from
Juba and forty miles from Nimule, Joseph Lagu, the son of a lay
teacher in an Anglican mission, was educated first at the Akot
mission school and then at the Loka mission school, before qualify-
ing to attend the Rumbek secondary school. When the Rumbek
school was moved to Khartoum in 1956, Lagu went with it. On
leaving this secondary school in March 1958 he applied to study law
at the University of Khartoum, and a few weeks later he also applied
for a place at the military college. He told me that he was accepted
by both, so he chose the one that commenced earliest, the Military
College, which he entered in July 1958, and so he became a soldier
instead of a lawyer. Commissioned into the army on the 1st May
1960, he was assigned to the '10th brigade' in the Northern Command as a 2nd lieutenant. He would then have been about twenty-
eight years of age, rather old to be a subaltern officer and to begin
a military career. His first posting was to Shendi, after which, in July
1960, he was sent to a battalion at Malakal, staying there only briefly
before going to one of its companies stationed at Juba. On arrival
in Juba he found the company had moved to Ikoto, so he followed
it there, and his first taste of 'command' was of a detached platoon,
some forty miles east of Ikoto. In October he was sent back to Juba,
and in February 1961 the whole battalion returned to Shendi, where
he remained.

On the 4th June 1963, while on leave in the south, he defected to the Anya-Nya, exchanging his rank of 2nd lieutenant, which he still was,[1] for that of colonel. He explained to me that 'The political situation at that time made southerners regard the army as a force to suppress their political aspirations. Units in the south were never looked on as a national army but as an army of occupation. If that was the situation, I could not remain in a force that was used to suppress my own people. I felt better to belong to the side of one's people, so that one is not sent against one's people and not looked at by one's people as a stooge.' His initial post was that of Secretary of Special Functions, which he himself told me he likened to that of a Minister of Defence, working with General Tafeng and the politicians who still had some authority in the Anya-Nya movement. For a year he was responsible in this role for the whole organization, and to the then leaders of the movement, until October 1964, when it began to splinter. Lagu then took over the eastern Equatoria region, and built up an efficient, self-contained, independent regional command. The reason for his abrupt defection has never been clearly stated, or what act or slight prompted him to change sides, but the carrot of rank, coupled with political acumen and ambition, cannot be overlooked.

Lagu had a pleasant personality, was intelligent and energetic, but he lacked the breadth of formal military education and experience. A leader who naturally attracted followers, he was an anti-Communist who favoured a Western-type democracy. Lagu personally told me that from December 1968 he began to work independently without taking instructions from any political leaders, and that 'the Anya-Nya gradually grouped around me, and politicians, seeing they were deserted, systematically all dissolved their parties and governments in exile, and left me to continue the struggle. Others gave their moral support, and others simply kept quiet.'

In October 1969 he formed the Anya-Nya High Command Council when, according to Lagu 'unity was almost complete', and its objects were, he said, 'to control and direct the operations, to search for military materials and distribute them, to administer the civilian population in areas under Anya-Nya control'. This Council met once a year. Indeed, during the latter part of 1969 the armed forces of the several southern 'governments', such as they were, struggled against

[1] Lagu explained to me that he was only gazetted a lieutenant while on the leave from which he did not return, and so he never wore his 'second pip'.

each other for recognition and supremacy, expending far more energy in this way than in fighting against the Government forces.

However, it was not until June 1971 that the ANAF High Command Council met for the first time, and even then the Commander of the Bahr el-Ghazal province was unable to reach the meeting-place in time. He did not arrive until his fellow Commander of the Upper Nile province had departed. The actual place of the meeting is not yet released by the southerners, but General Lagu told me it was, of course, at 'Owiny Ki-Bul' (the now customary reference to GHQ wherever it was situated).

Lagu's main opponents were the southern politicians in exile, who wanted to gain control over the Anya-Nya and who saw in Lagu the most likely person to unite the guerilla army. But Lagu felt that they were of no benefit to the struggle, and so he ignored them. Autonomous in eastern Equatoria, he kept aloof, although at one stage, after initial differences, he liaised with Joseph Oduhu; Oduhu in Kampala somewhat optimistically claimed that the Anya-Nya in Eastern Equatoria was under his political control. For months Lagu had been engaged in a struggle for authority with his nominal military superior, General Tafeng, but Lagu was working from a secure guerilla base.

Having consolidated his personal position in eastern Equatoria, Colonel Lagu turned his attention to uniting the Anya-Nya under his command, and began with the failing Anyidi Revolutionary Government, whose tiny army, momentarily commanded by Rolf Steiner, was cooped up in a small area in southern Equatoria, pressed on one side by the small group of guerillas of the Nile Provisional Government armed forces and on the other by Lagu's Anya-Nya in eastern Equatoria. Lagu's first victory in this power struggle was to bring about the collapse of the Anyidi Revolutionary Government, which occurred in April 1970, when he persuaded General Tafeng, and Tafeng's deputy, Colonel Frederick Magot, to join him and to place such forces as they could muster under Lagu's overall command. This was the first stage of Tafeng's being pushed into obscurity. Colonel Magot became Lagu's chief of staff, with a seat on the Anya-Nya High Command Council, which Lagu was shaping to suit his own plans and ambitions.

Next, in June 1970, Colonel Lagu engineered a coup against the Nile Provisional Government, which was headed by Gordon Mayen and based at Yei, in western Equatoria. First he won over Colonel

Samuel Abujohn, its chief of staff, whom he formally appointed commander of the western Equatoria region. Abujohn placed his Anya-Nya element under Lagu's overall command. On the 23rd May 1970 Stephen Lam, Mayen's Minister of Information, announced that because Gordon Mayen had failed to attract the southern politicians to his banner, he had 'disbanded his government' and intended to work to establish a National Liberation Front, led by Anya-Nya forces; this was a reversal of the usually accepted democratic principle that the military, even in war, must be subordinate to the civilian government. It was also a great triumph for Colonel Lagu, who had by this time gathered all effective military and political power in the south into his hands.

Lagu spent the latter part of 1970 in winning over more adherents to his personal leadership and consolidating his authority over the whole of the ANAF. His success was such that he was able to call a meeting[1] in August 1971 of military and political leaders, at which he announced the formation of the Southern Sudan Liberation Movement (SSLM), of which he became the head. He also promoted himself major-general, and additionally took on the post of commander-in-chief of the whole of the ANAF, thus holding in a dual capacity the top military and political appointments. Colonel Abujohn became his deputy, and Tafeng was pushed out, to take no further part in events, returning to his village in Latukoland.

Lagu explained to me that after he had assumed complete command over the Anya-Nya, he was not in favour of declaring a government in exile, or forming a political party in the south, but that he concentrated upon 'building and developing armed resistance'. However, pressure arose during 1970 from southerners, both in exile and in the south, for a political movement to be organized in conjunction with the ANAF. Lagu still resisted, and it was only after some secret contacts had been made with the Khartoum Government that he agreed. Present at this momentous meeting were Mading de Garang, representative of the movement in London, Lawrence Wol Wol, its representative in Paris, Lagu, and some GHQ staff officers.

From his GHQ at Owiny Ki-Bul, in the Immatong Mountains, until he was pushed out by Government troops, General Lagu kept a personal hold on the ANAF in eastern Equatoria, but as he gained authority over other elements of the Anya-Nya his grip tightened,

[1] Lagu told me 'in a place not yet to be mentioned' at Owiny Ki-Bul.

and weaknesses and shortcomings were rectified. Lagu gained full control of the illegal arms supply that filtered across the frontiers, and he doled out weapons and ammunition with discretion, being quick to withhold them if there were insubordination, suspicion of regional independence or plain banditry. The ANAF in Upper Nile province was commanded by Colonel Akwon, who had risen from the rank of private soldier during the course of the struggle, and in the Bahr el-Ghazal province by Colonel Emmanuel Abur, both of whom declared their allegiance to General Lagu.

Although efforts had been made to organize a civil administration in the territory under Anya-Nya control and influence, to establish courts of justice, schools and medical centres, results had been patchy, dependent upon local resources available and the energy and ability of local commanders. General Lagu set about regularizing and improving these aspects, appointing Elisapana Mulla, a former southern government official, to be Commissioner for Equatoria to organize a civil administration based on the old British pattern. Mulla also started a civil administration training centre at Langayu, about forty miles from the Uganda border.

A few prominent southern politicians in exile, and from former southern 'governments', agreed to work under Lagu, and were appointed to what might be termed ministerial-type posts. One of these was Aliaba Loboka Surer, former Minister of Finance in the defunct Anyidi Revolutionary Government, who became Commissioner for Education, and who set about organizing small forest schools of about 200 pupils each. A teacher training centre was also established, but there was an acute shortage of paper, books, teaching aids and equipment. Another, Felix Ibui, an experienced medical assistant, was appointed Commissioner of Health, and he began to establish forest dispensaries and small medical posts, as well as starting a medical training centre for personnel to staff them. His problem was the almost complete absence of drugs, medicines and equipment.

A little later General Lagu appointed Elia Lupe, a member of SANU, Chief Commissioner of the South, to be the highest civil authority, while Elisapana Mulla, who had done so much to put the civil structure on a sound footing, was appointed Commissioner for the Upper Nile province. The post of commissioner for the Bahr el-Ghazal province was left vacant, while Dishan Ojwe was appointed Police Commissioner. Soon General Lagu had what was virtually a small government functioning under his control. He also made contact with prominent southerners abroad, some of whom had been representing the south in their own way, or acting for their own parties or 'governments', and he formalized the representation of the SSLM. The principal appointments were that of Mading de Garang in London, Lawrence Wol Wol in Paris, Dominic Mohammed in Washington, Angelo Voga in Kampala, and Job Adlier in Addis Ababa.

Concurrently with the organizing of a civil structure in the south, and of uniting and training the ANAF, the military campaign against the northern troops in the south had to be continued. The Sudanese security forces were now better equipped with aircraft and helicopters. While the ANAF was better trained and disciplined than ever before, there were still frequent incidents of indiscipline, causing constant allegations from the Khartoum Government that the conduct of the Anya-Nya was not good. The northern allegation that southerners still did not take prisoners, but shot all northern soldiers they laid hands upon, was still largely true, although General Lagu tried to modify this practice.

Lagu's GHQ at 'Owiny Ki-Bul', wherever that happened to be, became the target for airborne assaults, some involving commando companies of northern troops, when rockets were fired from helicopters. There were southern allegations that the commandos were Egyptians. On the 25th January 1971 it was claimed that MiGs and helicopters machine-gunned and rocketed villages in the area of Magawe, in the Palwar Region, in eastern Equatoria, where a forest hospital was destroyed by aircraft action.

In February there was another airborne raid on Owiny Ki-Bul. It was unsuccessful but the Anya-Nya admitted to losing 12 men and much equipment. The southerners alleged that Soviet personnel had accompanied Sudanese army units into battle on this occasion. The Russians certainly involved themselves in ground operations but to what extent is not known. According to Government military sources there were at this time about a dozen Anya-Nya camps scattered about the south, which were the regional HQs. Government troops had moved in to occupy the real Owiny Ki-Bul. Later, President Numeiry allowed the encampment to be used by pro-Milton Obote followers. In July 1971 the southerners alleged that a school principal, a southerner, was killed at Akobo, a small town in Upper Nile province, near the Ethiopian border, causing the local

Anya-Nya to launch a punitive assault on the town's police post. However, in reprisal, the army took out 39 southern prisoners and shot them.

Beginning in 1971 the southerners alleged that Government troops changed their terrorist tactics from open killings to kidnapping individuals, taking people from their homes, killing them, and throwing their bodies in the river so that 'outlaws' could be blamed for the crime. In 1971 a Government spokesman claimed that the army in the south had a 'negroid' majority, consisting not only of 'Negroes from the Nuba Mountain area', but also southerners. Major-General Mohammed Abdul Gudir, Chief of Staff,[1] said that there were 3,000 southerners serving in the southern command, and that since the revolution of 1969 southerners had reached the rank of colonel.

The flurry of small guerilla-type actions continued relentlessly, and an Anya-Nya operations bulletin for July–August 1971[2] is a good example of the scope and type, although it is not possible to test the accuracy of the claims. It claims that despite the limitations of the rainy season the Anya-Nya maintained constant pressure on the Sudanese garrisons and vehicles in transit in Equatoria and Upper Nile throughout July and August, and that reports arriving from Bahr el-Ghazal indicated heavy fighting in that province. Retailing a 'Selection of Combat Reports', it reports that 7 vehicles were destroyed and 7 more hit in the eastern section of Equatoria, the main attacks taking place near Torit; that in the central sector 15 'enemy' vehicles were destroyed and 4 casualties incurred when a Government army post at Aula was attacked; that at Morta, which had previously been evacuated after a 'month-long' battle, the Sudanese troops evacuated the base, while in the western section a bridge was damaged by the Anya-Nya. In Upper Nile the Arab camp at Akobo was twice shelled and several buildings were burned, and in Bahr el-Ghazal it was claimed that there had been extensive Anya-Nya activity. It went on to list some of the 'major' actions and their results. The picture shown was one of mined roads and bridges, making the Government security forces even more dependent upon aircraft and helicopters.

In October 1971, at his second Anya-Nya High Command Council conference, chaired by General Lagu (who now signed himself 'Major-General Joseph Y Lagu, Commander-in-Chief of the Anya-

---

[1] On the 22nd December 1971.
[2] Shown as Appendix A

Nya Armed Forces and Leader of the Southern Sudan Liberation Movement'), several decisions were taken. Probably the most important was the dismissal of Brigadier Samuel Abujohn, the Deputy Commander-in-Chief and Commander of the western Equatoria region, because he had 'developed an unco-operative attitude to the command, lacked seriousness for his work, and had been accused of insubordination'.[1] Other southern sources indicated that Abujohn had plotted unsuccessfully to overthrow Lagu and take his place. Abujohn was replaced by Colonel Joseph Akwon, Commander of the Upper Nile Region, who was promoted to brigadier, and appointed Deputy Commander-in-Chief, but he still retained his regional command, while Lieutenant-Colonel Habakuk Soro, the Deputy Commander of the western Equatoria region, was promoted colonel and appointed to command that region.

The Anya-Nya High Command Council now consisted of General Lagu, as Commander-in-Chief, Brigadier Akwon as Deputy Commander-in-Chief, Colonel Frederick Magot as Chief of Staff and Secretary, and Colonels Abur and Soro. The next step in formalizing the ANAF was to divide it into three territorial brigades, which were the 1st brigade, commanded by Colonel Magot, consisting of all the Anya-Nya in Equatoria province, the 2nd brigade, consisting of all the Anya-Nya in the Upper Nile province, commanded by Brigadier Akwon, and the 3rd brigade, commanded by Colonel Abur, consisting of all the Anya-Nya in Bahr el-Ghazal province. The Equatoria region remained divided into three parts, the eastern, his power base, personally controlled by General Lagu, the central, looked after by Colonel Magot, and the western by Colonel Soro.

After July 1971 President Numeiry began secret diplomacy to try to persuade adjacent countries to stop supplies passing through them to reach the Anya-Nya and to cease providing southern refugees with a sanctuary, but he had less than moderate success, as old suspicions still lingered; the Sudan gave sanctuary to several groups of political exiles. The most serious differences in this respect were between the Sudan and Ethiopia, and despite frequent protestations of friendship and the occasional state visit, they did not improve in practice. Trying once again, Numeiry made a state visit to Ethiopia in November 1971. This was returned by Emperor Haile Selassi in January 1972, and eventually resulted in a belated agreement over southern 'outlaws' and Eritrean 'rebels'. The other country which

[1] The *Grass Curtain*

allowed supplies to pass across its territory to the Anya-Nya, and which gave sanctuary to southern refugees in number, was Uganda, but these facilities had been considerably reduced under the regime of Idi Amin, as he sought to improve his image and standing with Arab states. His predecessor, Milton Obote, was still in Dar-es-Salaam, which perhaps did something to influence Amin to continue to allow a trickle of supplies through to the south.

Beginning in December 1971, the Khartoum Government launched a military offensive in the south, the main object being to prevent the Anya-Nya activities spreading over and developing in the Bahr el-Ghazal province where, as compared with Equatoria province, there had been few guerilla incidents. The north had maintained almost constantly, for many months, three brigades, totalling over 14,000 soldiers, and about 6,000 armed police, in the south, and these were slightly reinforced.

The main Government thrusts were made south-westwards in the areas of Yei and Rumbek, and the Anya-Nya generally gave way before them in true guerilla fashion. Northern troops followed closely and chased the guerillas across the border into Uganda. On the 15th December an official spokesman at Kampala stated that fierce fighting was taking place just inside the Uganda border, but on the next day, the 16th, President Amin said that the Sudanese troops had been withdrawn. He added that he was inviting a Sudanese delegation to discuss the matter, and that he was willing to establish closer relations with the Khartoum Government, but it was not until the 27th January 1972 that belatedly Peter Gatwoth, a southerner, who was Numeiry's Minister for Southern Affairs, made contact in Kampala. On the 31st January the Government announced that in an attack in Upper Nile province 16 'mutineers' had been killed and a stock of arms and ammunition captured.[1]

On the 5th January 1972 the camp at Owiny Ki-Bul was attacked at 2200 hours by a group of Anya-Nya using mortars, light machine-guns and rifles, but the Government troops beat off the assault. There was a second similar attack about a fortnight later, but as the Anya-Nya fighters moved in they were fired at by the Sudanese soldiers, after which they withdrew. At this time Owiny Ki-Bul camp

---

[1] On the 22nd December 1971 General Lagu announced that he was 'freeing' 28 civilians, all Sudanese, whom he claimed to have rescued from a Sudanese Airways aircraft that crashed near Juba on the 6th December on a scheduled flight, the Canadian pilot being killed, and some of the survivors injured.

housed Ugandan political exiles, but was guarded by a detachment of Numeiry's soldiers.

On the 3rd March 1972 President Numeiry ordered his troops in the south to cease fire, and on the 6th General Lagu gave a similar order to his Anya-Nya, but the fighting continued on until the last minute, after which the military struggle formally came to an end.

12 *The Cease Fire and Afterwards*

'The present peace rests on a heap of sand with water
running underneath.'
                    Mohammed Ahmed Mahgoub in a private interview
                                        with the author, 23rd May 1974

Despite the overt intensity of the fighting between the Government
security forces and the Anya-Nya, especially in December 1971 and
in the opening weeks of 1972, delegations from both the north and the
south had been conducting secret negotiations since May 1971
through the good offices of the World Council of Churches, while the
UN High Commissioner for Refugees and others also helped. These
were brought to a head in February 1972, when the two delegations
met in Addis Ababa. The Government side was led by Abel Alier, a
Vice-President and Numeiry's Minister for the South, while that of
the south was headed by Izbone Mendiri, a former minister in the
Khalifa Government in 1964 and an exile since 1965, who had headed
the short-lived Sudan-Azania Government and was neither a member of the SSLM nor the ANAF. Within the southern delegation
Enoch Mading de Garang represented the SSLM, and Colonel
Frederick Magot the Anya-Nya.

On the eve of these talks Major-General Khalid Abbas, the Defence
Minister, resigned on the 13th, and the Chief of Staff on the 19th; both
were thought to be against the negotiations. Also, on the 17th, Major
Zeid, Secretary-General of the Sudanese Socialist Party, resigned, an
act which prompted President Numeiry to say that if there were any
more resignations he would dissolve the executive committee of the
SSP.

Negotiations almost foundered as soon as they began, as the
southerners firmly demanded a separate army, claiming it to be
essential as they were not convinced that northerners would be able
to protect them against reprisals. Emperor Haile Selassie stepped in
and called all the delegates to his palace, where he personally, and in
the name of the OAU, guaranteed the well-being of the southerners.

The southern delegation was persuaded to abandon this demand, and in turn the Government agreed to grant a greater degree of autonomy than it had at first intended.

After ten days' negotiations an Agreement for Autonomy for Southern Sudan within the Republic of the Sudan was reached on the 26th February 1972 and was initialled on the 28th. Brief details are to be found in Appendix B. There was to be an interim Government for eighteen months, after which elections were to be held for the regional assembly. On the 27th February Gordon Mayen, leader of the National Liberation Front, in exile in Zaire, denounced the agreement, describing it as an Arab fraud agreed to by southern delegates representing only themselves. The Government of Zaire promptly expelled him, and he moved to Belgium. Later he was invited to return to the Sudan by Numeiry, but declined. The most important person to be consulted was Major-General Lagu, Commander-in-Chief of the ANAF and leader of the SSLM, who after listening to reports by the southern delegates agreed to autonomy within the Sudan saying, on the 1st March, that he was 'in general terms quite satisfied', and adding that the majority of the Anya-Nya leaders also welcomed it.

On the 3rd March 1972 President Numeiry formally issued a decree granting autonomy to the south 'within the framework of the Republic of the Sudan', declared a general amnesty for all southerners who had taken part in the 'rebellion' and stating that he had ordered his armed forces to cease fire. Despite Lagu's remarks, not all the southerners were content to accept autonomy; many wanted complete independence, and the Anya-Nya themselves were under the impression that that was what they had been fighting for all these long years. It was not until the 6th March that General Lagu felt able to order the ANAF to cease fire, which they did, but in many cases reluctantly—the fighting continued right up until the deadline. Credit is due to Lagu for being able to persuade personalities and elements of the SSLM and the ANAF to accept this agreement. To give the southerners confidence in the Government's promises, President Numeiry, accompanied by Abel Alier, his Minister for the South, began, on the 5th, a ten-day tour to explain the terms of the agreement and to meet the people.

The original date for the ratification of the Agreement had been the 12th March, but Lagu asked for more time as he had to allay the doubts and suspicions of some of his supporters. Ratification did not take place until the 27th, at Addis Ababa, in the presence of Haile

Selassie, who had done so much to bring about agreement between the two sides. General Lagu said that his supporters would co-operate fully once they were recognized as full citizens of the Sudan. About one million southerners worked in the north, many of whom lived in shanty towns and squalid conditions, and their complaint was that they were always treated as second-class citizens. Lagu uttered a warning against eventual Sudanese accession to an Arab federation and, indeed, the settlement had been a set-back for Sudanese pan-Arabists. However, Numeiry made changes in his Government, removing pro-Egyptian and pro-Arab ministers, replacing them with men who took a softer line with the southerners. He brought in two southern ministers, Lawrence Wol Wol, who latterly had been the SSLM representative in Paris, and Samuel Nobay.

On the 19th President Numeiry formally promulgated the amnesty, and on the 20th lifted the state of emergency in the south, which had been in force since the 12th August 1955. An international commission to oversee the cease fire and the arrangements for the repatriation of refugees was composed of observers from Ethiopia, Kenya, Uganda, Zaire, the International Red Cross, the World Council of Churches, the UN High Commissioner for Refugees, and others.

On the 6th April President Numeiry appointed Abel Alier to be chairman of the Provisional Executive Council, which was to administer the south until a regional assembly could be elected. The Council was to consist of twelve members, who were nominated. It turned out to be a 'wide-range mix' and included the three governors of the three southern provinces nominated by Numeiry, Luigi Adwok, Tobi Madot and Hilary Logale, who were ranged alongside Joseph Oduhu, now prominent in the SSLM; Michael Tawili, leader of the defunct Sue River Revolutionary Government; Izbone Mendiri, who had headed the 'Sudan-Azania Government'; Elia Lupe, the SSLM's Chief Commissioner; Mading de Garang, and others whose names have been mentioned in this narrative. Of the other southern personalities, Aggrey Jaden became the Executive Director of National Resources of the South, and Clement Mboro became chairman of the Committee for the Repatriation of Refugees.

According to the agreement, about 6,000 Anya-Nya personnel were to be absorbed into the Sudanese armed forces in their current rank, and the remaining 4,000 were to be taken into the police, the prison service or their former occupations, it being thought in February 1972 that the strength of the ANAF was about 10,000.

The strength of the Sudanese army in the south was given as 15,000, which for a transitional period was to be placed under a commission of equal numbers of northern and southern senior officers, responsible to the central government. It was planned that the army in the south should be reduced to about 12,000 men, of whom half were to be northerners and the other half southerners. Additionally there were to be an armed police force and a para-military force of frontier guards, between 2,000 and 3,000 strong, all to be southerners.

However, on the 12th June 1972, it was claimed that the strength of the Anya-Nya was really between 25,000 and 30,000 strong, the majority of whom wanted to be absorbed into the armed forces 'at their current rank'. The Anya-Nya, who had retained their weapons (which proved to be mainly British rifles, Soviet grenades and Czechoslovakian automatic weapons), remained in the forests in their military formations, and were beginning to become impatient. Eventually a figure of 12,000 was agreed upon, and a six-year integration plan was worked out, in which for the first two years there were to be separate southern units with all-southerners in the ranks; then, in the next two years, southern sub-units were to be incorporated into northern units and vice versa; while in the last two years total integration was to be achieved. General Lagu produced a list of 'his officers', who were then 'rubber stamped' by a selection board, after which they attended special refresher courses to bring them up to the standard of their opposite numbers already serving in the army. Those who failed were given another chance and eventually the great majority of Lagu's Anya-Nya officers were accepted into the Sudanese armed forces in the rank they claimed to have held in the ANAF. A similar programme of selection and refresher courses was carried out for those claiming to have been warrant and non-commissioned officers in the ANAF. It was also agreed that a somewhat identical programme of assimilation should be practised in the police, the prison service and the civil administration.

Conditions tended to be vague and chaotic in the south. All roads were bad and some impassable because they had been torn up to clear them of mines. Communication and transport were therefore difficult. No journalists were allowed in the south, which remained a closed area. The Sudanese GOC of the south, Major-General Fatlalla Hamid, worked closely with General Lagu, and together they toured, visited and spoke to the people, explaining and persuading.

The Sudanese Government undertook to facilitate the return of refugees of whom, according to figures issued by the UN High Commissioner for Refugees in August 1969, there were estimated to be about 200,000; of these 70,000 were in Uganda. By April 1973 he was able to announce that the repatriation of 180,000 southern refugees would be completed by the end of June that year. By mid-August the official Sudanese estimates were that 143,000 southern refugees had arrived back from Ethiopia, the Central African Republic, Uganda and Zaire. Voluntary repatriation was virtually completed, except for three refugee camps in Uganda not under UN control. On the 28th June 1972 the Sudanese and Ugandan Governments had signed a mutual defence pact, and it was obvious that President Amin's swing towards the Arab Muslim states tended to block off the south. Amin had received considerable economic and some military aid from Colonel Gaddafi of Libya, who sent aircraft and troops to help him repel an invasion from Tanzania of Milton Obote's supporters in mid-September 1972.

On the 19th July 1972 a conspiracy against Numeiry by members of the dissolved Umma Party and the Islamic Charter Front, which involved army officers, was foiled by the security forces, after which Numeiry criticized his ministers, saying that he was searching for the best way to a 'genuine democracy'. This indicated deep trends of dissatisfaction at Numeiry's decision to grant the south autonomy. On the 26th January 1973 it was announced that a retired brigadier, Abdul Rahman Shenan, and eleven soldiers had been arrested for conspiring to kill President Numeiry and others. It will be remembered that Brigadier Shenan had led his unit against Abboud in March 1959, forcing Abboud to accept him on the Supreme Council of the Armed Forces, and that later in May 1959 Shenan was imprisoned, but released in November 1964 with others. Shenan was elected to the National Assembly, but lost his seat in 1968, and then retired from the army. He was later sentenced to three years' imprisonment.

After ratification in April 1973 by the National Assembly of a presidential form of government, confirmation that the Sudanese Socialist Union was to be the only permitted political party, and approval of the agreement with the south, the Assembly reverted to a legislative and advisory function only. On the 8th May the new constitution came into force. To mark the occasion 47 political prisoners were released; they included Sadik el-Mahdi, a former Premier and the remaining living leaders of the dissolved Communist

Party, who had been arrested in July 1971. On the 7th all the ministers were dismissed, and a new 14-man Government was announced on the 14th, with President Numeiry holding the portfolios of Premier and Defence Minister. It contained no southerners.

During the last week in August 1973, when President Numeiry was away on a state visit to Algeria, there was unrest in Khartoum, Port Sudan and Atbara by students and others who demanded 'the return of the army to barracks in order to leave politics to politicians'. This led to a state of emergency being declared on the 5th September, which remained in force until the 9th of that month. Numeiry hastily returned on the 7th. The basic cause of the discontent was the Muslim objection to Numeiry's agreement with the south. The President declared on the 9th that he might have to carry out a purge of the SSU.

The 60-member regional assembly for the south was to consist of 30 members elected on a territorial basis, and elections took place in November 1973. Of the remainder, 27 were representatives of provinces, regions or professional bodies, and 3 were nominated. There was to be a 13-man executive, or regional government of the south, which was announced on the 22nd October, and which replaced the Supreme Council of the South. It was known as the People's Assembly of the South, or more simply as the Regional Assembly. At its first sitting, on the 15th December, Abel Alier was elected President.

During his nineteen-month tenure of governing the south, Abel Alier had considerable achievements to show. He resettled some 850,000 displaced persons, who included about 220,000 returning refugees; it was officially estimated that in all about 1,190,320 people emerged from hiding in the forests, or from exile, and that only about 31,000 still remained in Uganda, where most of them had struck new roots. Farmers and agriculturalists were given tools and seeds to help them restart cultivation, and work was commenced on improving roads and bridges, help being received from several countries.[1] Reconstruction progressed. Money was made available by the Khartoum Government; it was spending £S7·5 million on basic services to the south, £S4·9 million on central and regional development, and £S5 million as a special grant to the south in an effort to speed post-war rehabilitation. But the main factor was the atmosphere

[1] According to *Soldier Magazine* of June 1974, about 200 British sappers built a road bridge at Tonj, over the Tonj River, for which the squadron was awarded the Sudanese Order of Merit, presented by Abel Alier as a Vice-President of the Sudan and President of the People's Assembly of the South.

of confidence that was returning, which was due chiefly to the close relations and good liaison between President Numeiry and General Lagu, which seemed to radiate into the south, where both the written and spoken word were used to promote better relations. A notice frequently seen on posters, buildings and walls, in Arabic and English proclaimed: 'The North and South go Hand-in-Hand'.

On the 3rd February 1974 Major-General Joseph Lagu was appointed Inspector-General of the Sudanese 'People's Armed Forces', a post which, of course, did not involve direct command of troops. The man to whom so much was due in uniting the south and bringing about a peaceful solution had chosen to remain a regular soldier rather than go into the political field. But I was told privately that he was slightly disappointed, as he had probably hoped to become the Defence Minister.

Relations between Numeiry and Lagu, already good, continued to improve during the following months, until on the 26th October 1974 Lagu was appointed GOC Southern Command. It was a bold, magnanimous decision to put the former 'rebel general' back into his old territory and give him command of all the troops there, both northerners and southerners, most of the latter having been his old Anya-Nya Freedom Fighters. It was a great gesture of trust on the part of President Numeiry, made despite the fact that there had been riots involving deaths and bloodshed in mid-October.

13 *The Grass Curtain*

'The curtain [surrounding the South] is not iron, but grass.'
Mading de Garang

The war fought in the southern Sudan from 1955 until 1972 was a secret, silent and hidden one—one that was smothered by a grass curtain. It was a shadowy war of flickering silhouettes, of unreliable 'official' communiqués and of many allegations, supported by little evidence. For years few knew of its existence, let alone its progress, and fewer still even cared. Vague rumours wafted out from the south at times, telling of northern atrocities, of harassed refugees, of a scorched-earth policy practised by the Khartoum Government, and even of deliberate genocide, but they were ridiculed by the Sudanese Government, were unsubstantiated, and remained so as journalists were not allowed into the 'closed' south. Eventually a few Western journalists, after illegally crossing frontiers, penetrated areas held by the Anya-Nya, and returned to write stories about the 'rebel army' holding out in the forests of darkest Africa against the 'Arabs', of their sufferings, needs and ambitions.

Such reports as were published tended to arouse suspicions that they were exaggerated to produce the appearance of a scoop. They could not be checked, nor could they compete for attention with other African tragedies such as the wars in the Congo and Biafra, which had able propagandists to hold world attention and plead their particular causes. The extensive television coverage given to these other wars may have caused widely varying reactions but it ensured that they were not ignored. No television cameras penetrated the grass curtain in the dark south, and had they done so the course of the war might have taken a different turn.

For long the south had no voice to draw attention to its problem. A few propaganda periodicals briefly appeared, but they had small circulations and some were of poor quality. It was not until May 1970 that the Southern Sudan Association was formed in

149

London under the chairmanship of Brian Hugh MacDermot and with a committee of several prominent people interested in the south and in the war that was in progress there. Its declared object was to publicize the southern cause and to help southern refugees. This association's most important activity was to produce a readable quarterly journal, printed in English, which gained a wide distribution and did much to bring to general notice the plight of the south. It was called the *Grass Curtain*, and was edited by Mading de Garang, with Lawrence Wol Wol as the deputy editor for some months. Its declared objectives were to achieve unity and a national entity, and it was used by General Lagu to put forward his opinions, and also to tell the world something of the fighting and conditions in the south. But it came on the scene at the eleventh hour—had it appeared in 1955 it would most probably have affected the course of the struggle and its outcome.

In the first issue of the *Grass Curtain* the editor wrote, in explaining the title, that it surrounded the south and that 'The current struggle in the South Sudan has one principal objective—the ultimate destruction of this enveloping curtain—the annulment of the Arab policy of Arabization of the South. For behind that vulnerable curtain are hidden the worst enemies of mankind: war, disease, famine, poverty and ignorance. As the curtain is not iron but grass, it will not withstand a concerted effort of the African people to lift it, and as grass, "drying up is inevitable".' In his final issue in mid-1972 the editor wrote that the *Grass Curtain* had been essentially born out of a need to consolidate a badly divided camp, and that 'the response we received from Southern Sudanese all over the world was a success beyond our expectation. That publicity was needed, was clear.' The last sentence was the most vital. Publicity is essential in any struggle, to enlist aid and sympathy and to counter false propaganda. The south had no publicity until it was almost too late.

As is so often the case, the root causes of rebellions and revolts lie buried in long periods of injustice, repression, exploitation and neglect, and this was so in the south. But there were other reasons, one of which was the traditional contempt of the northerners for the southerners, whom they regarded as inferior, as slaves, which caused them to administer the south, when the British left, arrogantly and thoughtlessly. There was only one point of political contention in the north, and that was over Egypt and the degree of contact there should be with that country; the south hardly entered the thoughts of the Sudanese political leaders. Mahgoub told me that the causes of the rebellion in the south were the 'British policy of separation, missionaries playing on southern fears of the slave trade, and ignorance and misunderstanding in the north of the southern problem'. Two cultures met and clashed; the Muslim north tried to identify itself completely with the Arabs; the other, mainly animist (with small Christian and Muslim elements only), had affiliations with black Africa.

Another reason was southern ignorance and lack of education. General Lagu blames the British for this, alleging that they deliberately left the south undeveloped, so the southerners were hopelessly inadequate to administer or look after themselves when Sudanese independence was declared. The British administration had certainly vacillated between uniting the south with the north and making the south a black Christian buffer region against the spread of Islam from the north. Education had been left almost entirely to the Christian missionary societies, which with their slender resources, and their restrictions, could barely touch the problem of illiteracy. Consequently, as compared with the north, which had a large body of educated people, the south lacked enough educated people to provide good leaders, administrators and military officers.

When the 'last straws' provoked the Torit mutiny in 1955 the south had no popular leaders and no political unity, only a great deal of tribal disunity. The first period, from 1955 to 1963, which can be termed the period of guerilla survival, was one in which small groups of mutineers and deserters fled for safety into the forests with their weapons because they feared they would be killed or imprisoned if caught by Government troops, or at the best transported to the north. Apart from a general hatred, and during this stage considerable fear of the Arabs, few of them had much in common with each other. Groups gravitated together on a tribal basis and moved towards their tribal areas where they hid, existing by plain banditry and sometimes becoming involved in fighting tribal enemies. The Government referred to them at first as 'mutineers' and then almost consistently as 'outlaws'; that is what they were during this stage, and they behaved accordingly.

Their military value was doubtful. They had only been trained as infantrymen up to company level, with the accent more on drill than forest tactics. Formerly they were employed on guarding posts, installations and convoys, providing guards of honour, ceremonial duties at headquarters and patrolling. Their tasks had been to deal with tribal clashes and squabbles, but their doctrine was that of desert warfare. It is doubtful if any of them, including the handful of commissioned officers, knew or had thought about the teachings of Mao Tse-tung, which had burst upon the world a decade earlier, and was the military talking point of the time. Guerilla warfare, with its basis of the fighter 'fish' swimming in the 'sea' of the people had not reached them, which accounts for their early harsh treatment of their fellow southerners.

The south was still a tribal region, and a backward one at that, with tribal prejudices, fears and petty greeds very much in evidence, while the poverty usually led to cattle stealing, which in turn provoked violent tribal reprisals. There was no common language in the south, and English was understood only by the few who had been fortunate enough to attend a mission school. Political awareness, let alone political unity, had not yet evolved from the tribal society. The few southern politicians either endorsed the Khartoum Government's policy of integration, or were extremely careful what they said in case they were placed in detention, being unable to give a firm, rousing lead and still remain at liberty. The grass curtain muffled any noise within the south.

Overshadowing the whole southern problem was the fact that Egypt had never accepted the loss of sovereignty over the Sudan. Throughout the south ran a fear that in some way the Egyptians might on one pretext or another find their way back, when it was anticipated that their attitude towards the southerners would be even more harsh than that of successive Khartoum governments. Talk of federation between Egypt, Libya and the Sudan caused southern alarm, as it was felt that if such a merger ever materialized one state might feel obliged to come to the military aid of another in an emergency. Thus one day Egyptian and Libyan troops might enter the Sudan in such numbers as to be able to crush the Anya-Nya completely.

Most of the southern politicians fled from the south in December 1960. By this time a form of southern nationalist spirit began to emanate, although it could not yet be thought of as a strong surge of nationalism. Southerners were too ignorant, bewildered and divided for that to occur so soon, and it was not until 1963 that the Anya-Nya developed as an insurgent army, having expanded as 'mutineers' were released from prison in 1961. Self-appointed, or sometimes elected, colonels appeared in charge of small areas or regions, and a vague military framework began to show. General Tafeng assumed the appointment of Commander-in-Chief, commissions were bestowed, and ranks were regularized on the British pattern. The various Anya-Nya groups had a form of liaison with adjacent ones and with General Tafeng, but as yet there was little central authority and the local commanders were almost autonomous in their own areas. Hatred of the Arabs and distrust of the Khartoum Government were still the twin threads that stitched them loosely together, but they gradually became conscious of being southerners fighting against northern repression. Banditry, individualism, indiscipline, a total disregard for local populations and for the conventional rules of warfare still prevailed, prisoners, for example, being shot out of hand. During this period the Anya-Nya had no political guidance, control or training, and so its elements were able to maintain their semi-independent status.

The next stage began in 1965, when arms were illegally obtained from those in transit across the Sudan to the Congo, and were added to by those taken, or bought, from the defeated Simbas fleeing from that country. A few arms were also smuggled over national borders. Thus the Anya-Nya acquired teeth, and individual groups were enabled to take more aggressive action. In this period, which lasted until 1968, indiscipline and banditry remained rife, although the Anya-Nya organization became more formalized. The period can be regarded as a dark age, through which little reliable light shines, as events were not recorded and only hearsay tales, now passing into folklore, exist in the majority of cases. I have heard several differing versions of the power struggle for position and dominance in this dark age, in which only the shadowy outline of a slowly developing guerilla army is visible. Today many tongues are silent, and others have probably been silenced. The value of folklore in a work of this nature is minimal.

The year 1969 saw the formation of rival southern 'governments' and splits in the Anya-Nya leadership as this or that senior officer, with his group of soldiers, took to politics and veered to or away from one or other of the 'governments'. Politicians entered the south and were soon tussling amongst themselves for personal power and a share in the control of the ANAF. There had been little military action by the Anya-Nya since spring of the previous year, and there was not much more during 1969. The year 1970 is the significant one, in which the south's fortunes improved, and Colonel Lagu, Commander of the eastern Equatoria region, rose from obscurity. Lagu stepped forward to unite political and military elements under his leadership in the struggle against the north. It was also the year in which the 'voice of the south' was heard abroad. United under (now) General Lagu, with a nationalist aim, the Anya-Nya was brought under stricter central control, discipline was better enforced, and the High Command Council, under his chairmanship, was able to reach decisions and to ensure that they were carried out.

The military struggle between the north and the south was that of insurgent warfare, or guerilla warfare—the better known but generally less understood expression. Northern conventional forces tried to bring to battle, or even capture, the elusive Anya-Nya, who disappeared into the forests when Government troops approached. The immense distances, the huge forests, stretches of scrub and swamp, hindered the north, with its small army, few aircraft and few vehicles, and enabled the Freedom Fighters, as they liked to be called, moving on foot, always to keep one step ahead. It was the classic case of a conventional army, holding and garrisoning the population centres and endeavouring to keep the roads open, matched against guerillas who had the freedom of the countryside and were always elusive. The rebellion was mainly confined to Equatoria province, and according to Mahgoub rested on the numerous small tribes in that province.

The impression I gained from talking to some of the actual combatants on both sides was that there was a great deal of shadow boxing in which the shadows appeared more fearsome than they actually were. It was a shadowy war in which few blows found their targets, a war of many wild swings, of many cries of anguish and of many groans, but in which far less blood was spilt in battle than either side cares to admit. On the Government side the operations gave the impression of simply being large field exercises with live ammunition, while on the Anya-Nya side, with their ample warning of danger, they were able to fade away in leisurely fashion into the forest. Once General Lagu was asked how, if that were so, the Government could put on display in Khartoum weapons, equipment, ammunition and uniforms after an Anya-Nya camp had been occupied by Government troops. He replied that it should be noted that the exhibits were old, disused or useless, and that his Anya-

Nya 'did not like clearing up very much before they left a camp'.

That the Anya-Nya survived its first few years was due mainly to northern military weaknesses, and primarily to the small number of troops available to pacify such a huge area with limited communications. The number of northern troops in the south probably averaged between 12,000 and 14,000, being stepped up to the 18,000 mark for special operations. Some reports indicate that at times it was as high as 20,000, but this figure is doubtful. If, however, we assume that it was correct, and if we work on the British military assessment that it requires ten times as many troops to defeat any given number of guerillas (as was proved in the Malayan campaign),[1] then the north never had enough men in the field to cope with the Anya-Nya, which after 1963 were never less than 5,000 strong—although only a proportion of them were armed. Unlike the British in Malaya, who had ample air facilities, vehicles and ships, and well-trained soldiers, the Sudanese armed forces until 1970 were short of both aircraft and vehicles. Moreover, the Sudanese army was involved in politics, rent with factions, took part in coups, and was periodically purged, which had a distracting and devastating effect on the small officer corps. All military eyes and ambitions were focussed on Khartoum and not on the south. A substantial proportion of the army was retained in Khartoum to bolster up and protect the current regime. Service in the south was regarded as unpleasant garrison duty, and the military aspect of the southern problem was pushed under the carpet as much as possible, a fairly common attitude being that it should be contained but otherwise ignored.

From 1970 onwards the Sudanese armed forces had more aircraft, vehicles and guns, with which they endeavoured to capture the various Anya-Nya HQs and so deprive the ANAF of its leadership and bases. The north consistently denied random bombing of villages, insisting that only Anya-Nya camps were attacked by aircraft when they were detected and pinpointed. The southerners allege the opposite. Another point was the constant allegation by the southerners of the indiscipline of the Government troops in the south, but independent observers say that discipline was good in the Sudanese army and the officers had full control over their men. Perhaps, however, it was different in the south, and discipline might

[1] See *Malaya: The Communist Insurgent War: 1948–1960* by Edgar O'Ballance (Faber).

have been relaxed deliberately for short reprisal periods in the forests, especially before the grass curtain was penetrated.

The Anya-Nya had a number of inherent weaknesses. Looking at them coldly one wonders how the movement survived its early stages, but perhaps the explanation is the ineffectiveness of the northern troops, their discontent, arrogance and their small numbers. The first drawback was the lack of an officer class to rally and organize. Originally there were less than a dozen who had formerly held commissions in the Sudanese army, but this lack was gradually overcome by natural leaders arising in the field by sheer character and ability which in the circumstances overcame lack of formal education and military knowledge. One such person was Joseph Akwon, a private soldier in the Equatoria Corps, who had been forced as a 'mutineer' to take to the forests, where he rose steadily to the rank of brigadier. He was commanding the 2nd brigade in Upper Nile province, as well as serving as deputy Commander-in-Chief, when he was killed in battle only a few days before the cease fire.

Inferior military arms and equipment were another handicap, especially in the early days. Indeed, a large proportion of the Anya-Nya had to be content with native weapons such as spears, swords, machetes and bows and arrows. Even at the time of the cease fire it was thought that less than one-third had firearms, with only limited amounts of ammunition. Military organization was poor and make-shift, due partly to lack of trained officers and partly to the fact that they were in groups, often with a tribal emphasis, or gangs, that resisted being organized until the last possible moment. It was only after 1970 that General Lagu was able to put pressure on regional commanders to regularize their formations by the threat of withholding arms or ammunition.

The Anya-Nya had poor communications within their organization; they had no vehicles and all movement was on foot, which took time, or along the waterways, and it was not until the latter years that the HQs possessed radios. No food supplies came in from external sources, but the nature of the country enabled them to live off the land as they were in small groups and never in large concentrations for any length of time. Later, arms and ammunition and other military material trickled in from adjacent countries, but never was there a supply route that even vaguely resembled the famous Ho Chi Minh Trail adjacent to Vietnam in South-East Asia.

The Anya-Nya had no previous battle experience nor any knowledge of guerilla warfare; in fact, they existed by good fortune and learned by experience. Training camps were set up, as soon as the Anya-Nya began to expand, where basic courses of instruction were given. The Freedom Fighter had a poor sense of time and of timing, and could not understand that he, or his section, had to be at a certain point at a precise time to give covering fire, to move into an assault or to carry out some other action in co-ordination with other sub-units. Rolf Steiner's comments on this southern failing were scathing. Desertion was a huge problem. Inherent fear of hostile tribal districts caused the Anya-Nya to be reluctant to move from their own home areas. Petty jealousies over tribal matters and promotion caused arguments and disunity. The importance of working together, of remaining steady under fire, and of discipline never really sunk into the minds of these carefree, timeless warriors. The officers who, without any formal military education, rose in rank within the Anya-Nya, did not realize how and why discipline was instilled into an army. Lack of discipline, issued rations and money, led to banditry, when groups of the Anya-Nya descended on villages and took the food and cattle they wanted. It was a way of life that continued in some degree until the cease fire, although it was stultified by the civil administration of the SSLM, when it was established, which gave receipts for the goods requisitioned. Another handicap was the high death toll from disease, as medical facilities were practically non-existent.

Such medical work as was carried out was undertaken by medical assistants who had received some Government training before they had taken to the forests to join the Anya-Nya. Only one southern doctor, Clement Khamis, went into the south in 1965 but he stayed only briefly as he found it difficult to work effectively, not only because of the lack of drugs, medicines and equipment, but mainly because he was hampered by the quarrels of the southern politicians. He left for Kenya, where he still practises.

On the high command and political level the main drawbacks were the inability to interest outsiders in the southern problem. Both the UN and the OAU declined to interfere, and would deal only with refugees; both organizations were wary of becoming involved in another disaster after being recently bitten by the wars in the Congo and Biafra. The south had no developed resources, such as commercial mineral wealth, nor were there hints that it might have some desirable product such as uranium, chrome or copper.

Had that been the case big business might have intervened. As it had nothing valuable to offer the outside world in return, no one hurried to send vital supplies and medical stores to the south. Few were interested in this dark part of Africa. The World Council of Churches was an exception; it had an axe to grind but little money to spare, while its influence on world affairs and opinion was doubtful. Lack of experienced diplomats able to lobby in foreign capitals was a drawback, and resulted in little contact with foreign governments. Even such countries as Ethiopia, Uganda and Zaire, which had underlying causes of friction with the Khartoum Government, hesitated to help or intervene openly. Simply no one wanted to know the poor, ignorant and helpless south, because it was not to anyone's selfish advantage to do so.

The cost in human suffering is impossible to itemize. Both Government troops and the Anya-Nya ruthlessly killed captured prisoners and villagers suspected of helping the other side or merely of being obstructive. Villages were razed to the ground by both sides, and agricultural land was abandoned as the people fled into the forests. Casualties were caused by bombing, rockets and machine-gunning of villages and camps from aircraft in the latter years and also many died from malnutrition, neglect or from famine. The usual figure of 500,000 dead, perhaps compiled by the propaganda machines of Christian vested interests, is bandied about casually, but so far as I can see it has no solid foundation. Government sources dismiss it as grossly exaggerated and even the former Anya-Nya admit in confidence that it might be far too high. The only certainty is that a great many people were killed in this war and many more died because of it, but no one knows exactly how many. It is accepted that well over one million people were displaced, having to flee for their lives. Neither the Government nor the Anya-Nya have published their total casualty lists, and perhaps the ANAF do not really know what their losses were (they cannot, for example, differentiate between deserters and prisoners taken by the northern soldiers).

The financial cost to the Khartoum Government was great, and was a huge strain on its slender resources and shaky economy. After the cease fire Abel Alier was asked what the financial cost had been. He replied that 'It was a lot, as security alone cost £S12 million. All social and economic plans had to be suspended and administration ran at a loss of £S5 million annually.'[1]

[1] *Middle East International*, supplement on the Sudan.

The Grass Curtain

The one outstanding personality in the south was Joseph Lagu, who with little formal military training or experience proved to be a natural leader who effectively united the south. Had he not appeared and asserted his dominance when he did, the southern resistance movement might have fallen apart. Lagu was adept at masterly inactivity, calmly remaining in his firm base in eastern Equatoria while activity occurred all around him. Many tried to involve him, but he stood aloof and did nothing. Politicians tried to enlist him in their cause—but again he did nothing. General Tafeng tried to persuade him to attack Government troops, but Lagu did not comply with the orders. Unmoving, he watched others expending their efforts tussling against each other, until finally, one by one, they turned to him as a solid island of stability.

One can ask who won, and the answer must be that no one did. The north wanted complete integration but had to settle for southern autonomy, while the south, which had been fighting for independence, had to accept something less. It was a compromise that both were wise to make, although there were elements in the north and the south who were against the settlement. Mahgoub told me that when he was Premier he was prepared to give all nine of the Sudanese provinces autonomy, including the three southern ones, but only individually and not as a 'Southern bloc' which, he said, would be but the first step to secession. He also told me that Abel Alier was the architect of the agreement, and that he had made it to suit the south and not the north.

The next question is whether, if the two sides had remained inflexible and determined, the struggle could have dragged on interminably and, as it continued, foreign powers would have intervened by proxy. Pride and poverty are characteristics of the Sudanese people, so one must assume that it could have carried on endlessly. The Soviet Union was supplying aircraft, weapons and vehicles, and perhaps in riposte other nations antagonistic to Russia might have begun supplying the south, when a Vietnam-like situation could have developed as the morass of the forests sucked in more and more military equipment and personnel. America's problem of how to extricate itself from Vietnam was very much before the eyes of the world at the time.

One has to look back well over the centuries to find an example of a black nation making war on an Arab one. When this war began few, least of all the 'Arab' northerners, expected the blacks to stand up to them and fight back. The question is can, and did, they meet the Arabs on equal terms, and if so why have the blacks always been the slaves and the Arabs always the slavers? There were no large-scale battles, and few pitched actions of any duration to give some scale of measurement of military capability, so we do not really know. We have Rolf Steiner's derogatory remarks about the blacks' fighting ability but he was probably embittered for personal reasons and they must be taken with caution. Perhaps, because of better training, military experience, education and modern weapons, the Arabs would so far have the upper hand, but the fact remains that the Negroes stood up to the Arabs in the protracted stage of guerilla warfare, and that must be taken into account. If they are not yet equal in fighting capabilities they might be in time, and a black army is in fact being trained which might one day, if northern promises are broken, break away from the north and renew the fight for southern independence. Suspicion remains, and many southerners are apprehensive in case the cease fire is broken. General Lagu's ability to treat and work with President Numeiry is the key to a more secure future in the Sudan.

Appendix A

Anya-Nya Operations Bulletin: July-August 1971

A = General

1. Despite the limitations of the rainy season, the Anya-Nya maintained constant pressure on Sudanese garrisons and vehicles in Equatoria and Upper Nile throughout July and August.
2. Reports arriving from Bahr el-Ghazal indicate heavy fighting and large-scale operations by Anya-Nya forces there.

B = Personnel

Brigadier Joseph Akwon has been appointed Deputy Commander-in-Chief of the Anya-Nya by Anya-Nya Commander Major-General Joseph Lagu.

C = Selection of Combat Reports
1. Equatoria

(a) Eastern Section

During late July and August 7 Sudanese vehicles were destroyed by Anya-Nya mines and ambushes, and 7 more were hit, although their destruction was not confirmed. The main attacks took place near Okulu on the Torit–Magawi road, at a point 14 miles west of Torit, and at the Lohileri bridge on the Nimule–Torit road.

(b) Central Section

Fifteen enemy vehicles were destroyed by mines and ambushes at Kaya, on the Lainya–Maridi road, the Yei–Kajo road, the Juba–Yei road, and between Tali and Somaring.

Anya-Nya forces attacked enemy troops at the Papa bridge on the Juba–Yei road, at the army camp at Aula, and at Nugents Hove in the Loka region. In this last attack Anya-Nya forces suffered four casualties. At Morta, which had previously been evacuated by Anya-Nya forces after a month-long battle, Sudanese troops finally yielded to continuing Anya-Nya military pressure and evacuated the base.

(*c*) *Western Section*

On 18th July part of the Ringasi bridge was sabotaged by Anya-Nya sappers, under cover of attack.

2. *Upper Nile*

On two separate occasions in late July the enemy camp at Akobo was shelled by Anya-Nya forces, and several buildings were burned. The Sudanese garrison at Nasir was also shelled.

3. *Bahr el-Ghazal*

Couriers arrived recently at Anya-Nya Headquarters in South Sudan, bringing news of extensive Anya-Nya offensive activity in Bahr el-Ghazal province.

The following are among the major actions:

(a) Between 9–11th March 1971 heavy fighting took place in the Tead-Adol region. Approximately 200 enemy troops in 14 armoured personnel carriers (APCs) and an armoured car attempted to attack Anya-Nya forces. In a series of counter-attacks and ambushes, Anya-Nya forces destroyed 2 troop carriers at a point 27 miles from Wau on the Tonj–Wau road, and 2 more at a point 10 miles south west of Wau. Enemy losses were placed at 86 dead.

(b) In a second clash on 23rd March the Anya-Nya lost 1 dead and 2 wounded; the enemy losses were 12 dead and 1 APC.

(c) In an attack on the Sudanese position at Tiar-Aliet (31 miles east of Aweil and 29 miles west of Gogreal), Anya-Nya forces killed 21 enemy soldiers and policemen and wounded approximately 13. Anya-Nya losses were 9 killed and 14 wounded. Arms and equipment were also captured by the Anya-Nya.

(d) In two attacks, on 16th and 28th April 1971, the railroad to Wau was taken out of operation for several weeks. In the first attack the enemy lost 32 dead, and 10 railroad cars were derailed.

In the second attack 30 yards of track were destroyed and 4 railroad personnel were killed. Following this incident other railroad personnel refused to operate the line for several weeks.

An Extract from the *Grass Curtain*

Appendix B

Agreement for Autonomy for Southern Sudan within the Republic of Sudan[1]

The agreement's provisions include the following:

(a) Upon ratification of the agreement by President al-Numeiry and General Lagu, to take place in Addis Ababa on 12th March, a cease fire would come into force throughout the southern Sudan.

(b) The cease fire would be followed by the gradual establishment of regional autonomy, under which the three southern provinces of Bahr el-Ghazal, Equatoria and Upper Nile would be united in a Southern Region under its own Regional President.

(c) The Regional President would be chosen by an Executive Council, whose members would be appointed by the Sudanese Head Council upon recommendation by a Regional Assembly. This Council would control all aspects of southern policy except defence, foreign affairs, currency and finance, and economic and social planning, which would remain under the control of the, central Government in Khartoum, in which the south would, however, be represented.

(d) The Executive Council would be responsible to the Regional Assembly, which would be elected by universal adult suffrage within eighteen months of the ratification of this agreement.

(e) The Anya-Nya military forces (of about 12,000 men) would be incorporated into the Sudanese Army's Southern Command (then about 15,000 strong), which would, for a transitional period, be placed under the command of a commission of southern and northern officers (in equal numbers) responsible to the central Government; the army would gradually be reduced to 12,000 men

[1] Keesing's Contemporary Archives

(half northerners and half southerners) until the south set up its own machinery for maintaining law and order, for which it would have its own armed police force and 2,000 to 3,000 frontier guards.

(f) While the official language would be Arabic, English would be the 'common language' and be taught in schools in the South.

Initialled at Addis Ababa, on 28th February 1972

Index

Aba Island, 20, 22, 24, 63, 106–8
Abbas, General Khalid Hassan, 106, 126, 142
Abbas, Philip Ghaboush, 103
Aboud, General Ibrahim, 48–50, 52–7, 59, 61–8, 70, 73, 104, 112, 120, 146
Aboukir, Battle of, 19
Abdullah, Brigadier Moheiddin Ahmed, 54–6, 67
Abdullah, Mohammed Ahmed al-Mahdi, 22–3
Abiei, Gordon, 70
Abu al-Istiqal, 23
Abu Anga, 85
Abujohn, Colonel Samuel, 135, 139
Abur, Colonel Emmanuel, 136, 139
Accra, 78
Acholi tribe, 126
Addis Ababa, 92, 137, 142, 143, 163, 164
Aden, Brigadier Abdullah Mohammed, 106
Adlier, Job, 137
Adol, 162
Adwok, Luigi, 46, 67, 72, 76, 95, 114, 144
Africa(n)(s), 16, 20, 24, 28, 31, 47, 63, 82, 84, 87, 91, 94, 105, 117, 120, 126–7, 129, 149–50
Agar tribe, 18
Agreement for Autonomy, 143, 163
Ahmed, Colonel, 112
Ajulo, Colonel Nyingeri, 88
Akhbar al-Usbu, 93

Akobo, 88, 123–4, 137–8, 162
Akol, Peter, 74
Akwon, Brigadier Joseph, 123, 136, 139, 156, 161
Albanian detachment (Battle of Aboukir), 19
Albino, Oliver, 35, 59, 74, 81
Algeria(n)(s), 71, 73, 79, 129, 147
Aliab Dinka tribe, 26
Aliah tribe, 18
Alier, Abel, 15, 105, 114, 142–4, 147, 158–9
Alier, Bullen, 44
Aliet, 162
America(n)(s), 27, 45, 50, 78, 95, 101, 104, 106, 114, 117, 130, 159
American Missionary Publishing, 69
American Presbyterian Mission, 27
American United Mission, 27
Amin, Idi, General (President), 127–8, 140, 146
Amin, Brigadier Makboul al-, 55
Anglo-Egyptian Agreement (of 1953), 36
Anglo-Egyptian army, 24
Anglo-Egyptian Treaty (of 1936), 31, 36
Anglo-Sudanese Constitution Amendment Commission, 35
Angudri, 97
Ansar, 22–4, 27, 32, 44, 49, 65, 72, 104–8, 112
Anti-Imperialist Front, 46, 49, 65, 71

165

Index

Index

MacDermot, Brian Hugh, 150
Madi tribe, 59, 132
Madot, Tobi, 114, 144
Magawi, 137, 161
Magot, Colonel Frederick, 134, 139, 142
Mahdi(ists), 23–4, 27, 34, 47, 107
Mahdia, 22
Mahdi family, 101
Mahdi, Imam el-Hadi al-, 75, 90, 95, 100, 106
Mahdi Revolt, 22–5, 27, 32
Mahgoub, Abdul Khalik, 71, 93, 108, 110, 112–13
Mahgoub, Mohammed Ahmed (Premier), 18, 23, 59, 71–2, 74–85, 89–90, 92–3, 95, 100–3, 107, 118, 142, 151, 154, 159
Majok, Philemon, 76, 97, 100
Makboul, Major-General Abdul Rahman al-Tahir al-, 65–6
Malakal, 29, 41, 83, 131–2
Malaya(n), 155
Malek, 27
Malta(ese), 110
Mameluke(s), 19
Mandari tribe, 18
Mao Tse-tung, 86, 152
Marchant, Captain Jean-Baptiste, 24–5
Marial Aguog, 121
Maridi, 41, 81, 88–9, 130, 161
Martin, David, 127
Matika, 130
Mayen, Elijah, 46
Mayen, Gordon, 97–9, 115, 134–5, 143
Mboro, Clement, 66, 68–70, 76, 91, 95, 97, 100, 105, 113, 144
Mecca, 17, 19
Medina, 22
Meir, Golda, 126
Melut, 27
Mendiri, Izbone, 15, 46, 66, 69–70, 72, 98–9, 142, 144
Menelik, Emperor, 25
Middle East International, 158
Mide, 81

Military College, Sudanese, 40, 104, 132
Military School, Khartoum, 29–30
Missionary Societies Act, 52
Mobutu, of Congo, 71
Mogan, 115
Mohammed Ahmed (Madhi), 22–3
Mohammed Ali, 19–21, 26
Mohammed, Dominic, 137
Moli, 132
Molotov cocktails, 60
Mombasa, 88
Mongalla, 22, 26, 39
Morta, 122–3, 125, 138, 161
Moru, 97–8
Moru (tribe), 18, 59
Moscow, 110, 112, 117
Mount Kinyeti, 17
Muerwal, Dominic, 53
Mulla, Elisapana, 136
Muortat, Gordon, 72, 76
Murghani, Ali al-, 49
Murle tribe, 18
Muslim(s), 13, 23, 27–8, 30–1, 36, 39, 42, 48, 51–2, 60, 62–3, 75, 80–1, 83, 85, 127, 146–7, 151
Muslim Brotherhood, 101, 106, 108

Nairobi, 77, 81, 99
Nasir, 121, 124, 131, 162
Nasser, Gamel Abdul (President), 25, 36, 47, 56, 71, 103, 107
National Assembly, 25, 37, 40, 42, 44, 46, 48–9, 52, 61, 71, 75, 78, 93, 104, 146
National Front, 35
National Liberal Front, 135, 143
National Unionist Party (NUP), 35–7, 44, 46–7, 65, 71, 75, 78, 85, 90, 94–5
Nazi Storm Troops, 128
Nazra, 40
Negro(es), 13, 24, 28, 103, 138, 160
Neguib, General, 36
Nelson, Lord, 19
New York Times, 121
Nigeria, 73

170

DATE DUE	
APR 24 2000	

GAYLORD   PRINTED IN U.S.A.